FNL

Lessons from a rather full life

Bipolar, diabetes, cancer … what next?

Robert WILSON THOMAS
Co. Meath, Ireland, May 2022

Preface

This is a memoir of some events that brought me to where I realise that life prepared me for many of my current challenges.

I make no apology for my idiosyncrasies, nor the selection of events, nor an excuse for sharing them, nor for what they are. I am grateful for how they, with many people together have prepared and moulded me! I also make no apology for my English.

Whilst I may appear to be self-effacing or shallow, this is a patina and hides a shy, intense, personal, and self-opinionated human being, although I prefer to be thought of as a human *doing*.

But first as John F. Kennedy observed *"We must find time to stop and thank the people who make a difference in our lives."*

My gratitude includes many people who have made it possible for me to be me.

Diolch yn fawr iawn, pawb.

Contents

How did I get here?

A question that parents dread as a child grows out of belief in Santa Claus and develops embarrassing curiosity. This book does not the answer *that* question. The explanation is that in November 2016 I had what '*they*' assured me was a '*relatively minor*' operation to remove a tumour from a kidney. The surgery was expected to be two hours, with four days on a ward and a month to recuperate.

That was the theory, but '*Man proposes, God disposes*'.

Surgically, the operation a success, save that I learned from my medical notes, a year later, that they took part of my right kidney. Five years on and the cancer shows no sign of returning.

Post-op in the Recovery Room, a doctor assumed that a sudden rise in my blood pressure was due to internal pain despite, ten minutes before, I had confirmed I had no pain. He administered fentanyl and some minutes later, another medication which clashed and triggered something called Serotonin Syndrome. I collapsed, my heart and breathing stopped and I was rushed from the ward to intensive care.

I was revived, but two days later I had a second cardiac arrest and stopped breathing. After the first time my hands and legs began to thrash wildly. I was sedated but the thrashing didn't stop. I had a week in Intensive Care, in an induced coma, then three weeks on a ward. I have few memories of the early days, none is pleasant.

This was the start of my Functional Neurological Disorder (FND).

This book is to highlight elements of my fight to reclaim my ability to function as close as I can to my former life. It is a battle faced by hundreds of thousands of people with FND. In my journey to a new reality and my '*normal*' I have recognised that many things that help now, I learned, in different context, earlier in my life.

My fight is not over. It may never be, but I am eternally optimistic about the future.

A significant portion of proceeds from sales of the book will be donated to FND Hope, for the benefit of other sufferers with FND, world-wide.

Parents and Parenting

World, you were warned, 4th November 1952!

Home life

I was raised in a home where emotions, feelings or preferences were discouraged. My father was self-opinionated, controlling and overbearing, things he failed to recognise. I received scant praise or encouragement for what I wanted to do though they were lavished for '*approved*' activities.

Drummed into me was the Victorian idea that '*big boys don't cry*'. They do, a natural and healthy reaction to cope with stress. In recent years, after my father had kept me on a short emotional chain my entire life, something he delighted in jerking to the day he died, I have realised that my upbringing was Childhood Emotional Neglect.

I never lacked physical stuff. I went to a Scout Jamboree in Idaho and had a couple of school trips to France. We had foreign family holidays, much an exception to the norm.

Piano lessons were inflicted on me, based on the theory that an ability to play was a passport to free beer in any pub in Britain. It did happen, just once.

I taught myself the trombone and was in the school orchestra, ultimately leader of the brass section. Once I asked my father if he would come to a concert. He declined saying when he wanted to hear music, he would '*go and hear a proper orchestra*'. I never made the mistake of asking again.

I cannot remember his listening to my playing the guitar either, also self-taught. He did threaten to cut the strings if I played it, even quietly, after he had gone to bed.

I was starved of opportunity to express myself, as an individual. I often yearned understanding but rarely was it available. The absence of sympathy and understanding caused a lot of trouble for relationships as (if he disapproved) my father would find less than subtle ways to say so, even mocking a girl's physical characteristics. He would not say anything when it was plain to all (but me) that I was making a huge and wrong life decisions. His greatest failure was admitting, after my first marriage had disintegrated, that he 'had thought all along I was making a mistake'.

A good example of his lack of appreciation came after the launch party for my first book. Against the odds, he came to London for the bash. As we left, I said it had been the first time he had been introduced as my father, but previously I had always been his son. His response?

"What's the difference?"

Lessons from Parents and Parenting

Absence of emotional support and encouragement is as damaging and abusive as physical mistreatment, though the scars are deeper and mostly invisible.

Sometimes the best memories are, at best, memories. Some, possibly a majority, better are forgotten.

Education, School and afterwards

Education

Education is what's left over after you've forgotten all they taught you in school. Educate comes from two Latin words: '*e*' or '*out of*' and '*ducare*' or '*to draw*'. It is drawing out what someone knows or of what he or she is capable, rather than a process of learning irrelevant facts, that never may be needed or helpful, to be spewed out in an exam.

Schooldays were not the happiest years of my life. I endured them, under the impression that I was enjoying myself. In fact, I hated most of it.

My first school, Ty Coch primary was out of date when I went there, arriving kicking and screaming a week after my fifth birthday. I remember vividly that the clouds were tinged with ominous shades of red and grey. It was full due to the post-war baby boom. In the last year our teacher, Mr Smith, pressed us to master three skills: mental arithmetic (we had lots of practice), a firm handshake and a distinctive signature. I retain reasonable skills in all three.

I left Ty Coch to go to Bishop Gore Grammar School as had both my father and my grandfather. Its most famous pupil, Dylan Thomas was mentioned twice, neither in a lesson. Now there's a plaque commemorating him.

For many, Bishop Gore was a miserable place. I was told I was stupid and not expected to amount to much. Corporal punishment was rife, even commonplace, whether justified or not. I was often isolated and an easy target for bullying, even by prefects, mainly as, for some time, I was the only boy of 900 in shorts.

Contrary to the opinion of most staff and my fellows, I was reasonably intelligent, but never had an opportunity to demonstrate it. I accept I was not a perfect, nor even a fair pupil. I was hopeless at games, except swimming, until that stopped due to perforated eardrums. My redeeming virtue was a clear reading voice, so I was regularly in demand for reading passages in morning assembly.

It must have been a surprise to the staff when I passed nine O-levels (mostly lower grades) and then A-levels, in chemistry, physics and maths. My grades were enough to get me into Bath University to read chemical engineering, which, after medicine, veterinary science and law, was the hardest curriculum available. The choice was due to my liking science and that my Godfather was a chemical engineer. He suggested we talk about my career '*in a few years*'. I was in my second year at Bath when next I saw him, and his advice was well-meant but too late, quite minimal, and unhelpful.

Again, I was average, struggling to keep my head above water, but I had fun! After three years and despite my tutors' darkest predictions and my own efforts to enter academic oblivion, I achieved modest success with a lower second-class honours' degree.

I had known from early on that whilst the course was fascinating as an academic subject, I did not want a career in engineering. I had no idea of what I did want to do. My father suggested that I train as an accountant, a solicitor or a barrister. The first was unthinkable as Dad had come third in the country in his finals, so anything less than second would be failure. Life of a solicitor suggested tedium so by default I read for the Bar. In retrospect it was a happy choice and given my time again, I would follow the same path.

I knew as much about life as a barrister as I did about engineering. I had never been inside a court nor discussed a career in law. It seemed as good a way as any to spend another three years without working for a living. I arrived in London unaware of what to expect and spent three years stumbling through, doing just enough as prudent until I was called in July 1977.

I had two periods of pupillage, the Bar's equivalent of articles (working unpaid for a senior barrister to learn the ropes). The first six months was in a general set of chambers, doing criminal defences in everything from petty theft to armed robbery. Mostly it was in drugs. This was fine, but for seeing the suffering through over-zealous enforcement of the Misuse of Drugs Act. It brought home that some police officers, particularly in drug squads, were less than factually reliable.

After my criminal six months, I moved to become pupil to a remarkable man, Michael Fysh. This was in intellectual property (*collectively patents, copyright, trademarks, designs, trade secrets and confidentiality, a very specialised part of a small section of the legal profession*). This was my niche, the love of which I retained through my career.

Fysh and I co-authored a book, the Industrial Property Citator, a specialised reference with a plot second only to the London telephone directory, and useful only to a tiny market of intellectual property lawyers. Later I wrote two updates, a second edition (the Intellectual Property Citator) and two more supplements. A labour of love and of which I am disproportionately proud. They are still in print and together can be yours for about £500. Not a best seller, but it brings me a few bob a year!

THE INTELLECTUAL PROPERTY CITATOR

VOLUME 2
1982–1996

by

Michael FYSH, Q.C., S.C.
of the Inner Temple and King's Inns, Dublin
Barrister-at-Law
Barrister, Supreme Court of N.S.W.
Advocate, High Court at Bombay
and Supreme Court of India

and

Robert WILSON THOMAS
of the Inner Temple
Barrister-at-Law

London
Sweet & Maxwell
1997

Getting a seat in chambers is easier if you went to Oxbridge, rather than a new, redbrick, technology-oriented pile like Bath (then yet to establish itself as the darling of Sloane Square and Chelsea) and was well connected in legal spheres.

I was neither.

It was clear by the end of 1978 that I would not be staying. Thus, in spring 1979, I accepted a job in industry and in industry I spent my career, never regretting the decision to leave the Bar, nor ever wanting to return.

Lessons from Education

Life is an opportunity to learn. Everyone you meet can teach you something.

No learning or knowledge is without purpose.

Be mindful about everything.

When your chance comes, be ready and take it and enjoy every moment, even the bad ones. They are your lessons in life.

Career merry-go-round.

I was a career butterfly. After my first job, I had a clutch of others, most lasted but two or three years. I started as Patents Lawyer then Licensing Executive for a British engineering firm and after a spell as Intellectual Property Lawyer (a misnomer but my favourite job title) with the then second largest computer company in the world, I took the decision to step back and learn how to be an in-house general counsel. For five years I endured the mistake, serving as UK Legal Manager for a telecoms equipment company but learnt the trade. After three years with an airline reservation company taking part in a vast merger with its American counterpart, I drifted into a start-up company in the gas industry then found my feet as an external consultant, again in telecoms.

I was rather malleable, taking on such a range of responsibilities, and against the odds not making a complete ass of myself in any of them. Each gave me experience, for the collective sum of which I am most grateful.

The consultancy was the last UK post I held before I moved to Ireland for my final, paid job, European Counsel for a silicon chip company.

High points

There was a rite of passage, not being called to the Bar, which was a limp handshake from someone I had neither heard of nor met. It was the first time I was addressed in court, as '*My learned friend*'.

After so many and varied professional experiences, too many to recount, a few notables rank above the others.

Top of the list was leading a team in the Peace Stability Force, or SFOR, part of the Dayton Accord for Bosnia Herzegovina. My role was to revise the Broadcasting Law and practice.

My official SFOR ID Card.

After the Bosnian civil war, Dayton brought a fragile peace to the conflict. It did not alter deeply ingrained prejudices. There was an urgent need to establish order in broadcasting. After Dayton there were many reports of broadcasters spewing out hate language. I saw several transcripts, made by military intelligence, and the blatancy, crudeness, and thoroughly false claims, by all sides, still shocks me these years later.

The only remedy then was to confiscate equipment or to send in tanks to destroy transmitters and even buildings if resistance was met. Simple but effective, but it didn't silence the voices for long.

My team established a Controller General of Broadcasting. I drafted a new Broadcasting Act, a licensing regime, and associated Broadcasters' Codes of Practice. We made these accessible and inexpensive, so most signed licenses and followed the codes. Subsequent elections, the first open elections in Bosnia, were fair and free and there was not even one report of hate speech.

o-0-o

In 1998 or 1999, in Bucharest I presented a proposed law on telecommunications and data protection, which I drafted. This was the first time in ANY former Soviet bloc country that a new law was discussed with the public before it was implemented.

o-0-o

In my last job, I drafted, negotiated, and executed large volume software licensing agreements. These typically, were worth from about $20 Million to $150 Million. I would do ten to fifteen each calendar quarter, always at a rush due to a fiscal deadline and generally I worked by myself.

In one quarter I did seventeen such Agreements whilst seven colleagues in the US Legal Department managed eighteen between them. In three years, the combined value was well over $10 Billion. My responsibility was for words not numbers, so I never bothered to keep a tally. None ever failed, so far as I know.

Low points

There have been some, not all my own making.

The worst was my being dismissed from a job where I was significantly over-performing on the same day as my manager learned of my bipolar diagnosis. In my unfair dismissal case, he claimed that '*a manic depressive cannot be an in-house lawyer*'.

He was pissed off that I was better qualified and more able than he and that I got more praise and attention from senior management. Bipolar was used to eradicate the competition.

He lost the case and the company paid me handsome compensation, but I was not reinstated. Even if I had wanted to be.

Lessons from my career.

Dedication, an element of patience and an almost completely open mind pays dividends even if only these qualities are recognised in the longer run. Little is new, save for an occasional piece of legislation or a different jurisdiction.

You may never know your influence. One person can make a huge difference. This is as much to negative effects as to positive, though positive changes generally are more spectacular, significant and longer lasting.

Health and Wellness

Unhealth and the antidotes

Smoking

My first smoke was as a 13-year-old on a hike in Gower. I smoked occasionally over the next three or four years, at youth club and in university I smoked for a couple of months then with a new, non-smoker girlfriend, I gave it up. In London I resumed the habit, not for any good reason.

I smoked on and off until my mid-thirties. In 1983 I received a less than subtle hint that time had come to quit. This was from a blonde I was dating. One night as we slipped between the sheets she whispered: "*You smell disgusting!*" Her tone and expression confirmed it was not an offhand remark. She was very serious! As verbal foreplay it failed. As an incentive to quit it was effective. I forget the date of my last smoke save it was near the end of 1983.

On several occasions I had gone two or more years without a smoke, only to lapse. Bizarrely, for days before the end of the Tour de France Randonnée (about this, more later) and arguably at my peak strength and fitness, I had an urge, nigh on obsession for a French cigarette. I resisted until after finishing then bought some *Gauloises* and ended three years of abstaining.

I have now been an ex-smoker since 1983 with only an occasional, but completely resistible urge to light up.

Alcohol and alcoholism

My affair with drink started early. My father would allow me and my sisters a beer or a glass of wine with meals, particularly on foreign holidays. I liked the taste.

I drank in Uni occasionally getting blitzed at parties, but not habitually nor to excess. After I moved to London, social drinking was consistent with reading for the Bar, as to qualify you must eat so many dinners in Hall ('keeping term'). The dinners were subsidised by the Inn of Court and included wine and even port on Grand Nights. After dinner the rest of the evening usually would be in a pub near my Inn.

It developed to where all activities included provision for a 'wet'. Even long-distance cycling – 200 km or more – would include a pub stop during and almost always after. Justification was that I had *earned* it. Even training, out and back 100 miles or so, included lunch and a couple of beers.

Business trips were punctuated with drink. Transatlantic flights were fuelled by drinking. Once I returned to Gatwick from the USA, drinking steadily from take-off until the bottle of Champagne for breakfast. I poured myself off the plane to be met an hour or so later by my then girlfriend, whilst I was being guarded by a WPC who asked her "Does this belong to you?"

Many of my relationships were with women who also enjoyed a drink or three. It was a norm. Unhealthy but a norm.

My first marriage was orchestrated with drink. Rarely a day passed without drinking, but only to excess. My wife matched me, glass for glass. Drunken rows were regular. Towards the end despite our having a son under a year old it became very foolish. There was a bunch of like-minded people, hangers-on not friends, who encouraged consumption and used it to sponge drink off us. Group sessions ended after I left the marital home, but not the habit of beers in an evening and customarily a nightcap or two.

Around Christmas 1989. the abuse became obvious to me, though possibly not to anyone else. On several occasions I drank two bottles of wine and a half a bottle of spirits. Sometimes it was a complete bottle of spirits. I never had a hangover, nor difficulty concentrating the next day.

I was on lithium to control my mood swings and the lithium serum level must be monitored regularly to avoid liver function complications. Blood tests showed my level consistently near the lower end or below the therapeutic range. I was on the maximum dose and my shrink was concerned that control of my moods was failing.

On 28th December 1989, after a period where I had lost all recollection of few evenings, I decided to see if I could go without drink for a month, to see if I could.

The month passed, so the target became two months, then three. I realised I did not need to drink. My lithium level rose from below therapeutic to toxic. Medication was cut by 40%, where it stayed for twenty-five years.

I have not drunk alcohol since December 1989. I am an alcoholic in recovery. I may seem boring, even my father tried to cajole me off the wagon, without success.

There were some minor drawbacks. Being nominated driver was an inconvenience. A choice of beverage was another, though this has changed. Early on I resisted alcohol-free beers for fear that even a negligible alcohol content might be mildly intoxicating and tempt me back to drinking.

Vegetarianism

After a trip to Paris in 1990, for an interview which was an unmitigated disaster, I decided to spend a few days in France, to enjoy myself. I had a meat-heavy diet, including *burger de cheval frites* (yes, horse burger and chips!). On my return in Tesco's, I took a steak from the chilled meat section, looked at it and felt a wave of revulsion. I returned the meat with a resolution *"I will never eat meat again!"*.

A limited choice of foods if out was the only bugbear, but this has changed over the last 30 years. It is now OK to be veggie and if I lived alone, I would probably eat a mainly vegan diet.

Diet

Despite being meat-free, I eat fish.

In recent years, a nutritionist was concerned that I did not seem to have enough protein. Also, after my FND kicked off, I lost about 20% of my body mass. My clothes hung loosely off me!

These together lean towards my bolstering breakfast with a smoothie of flavoured whey protein powder (tastes better than it sounds) and I add nuts, sunflower and other seeds to cereals or porridge. My weight has been reasonably constant for a few years which is a relief.

I also have a mug of hot milk with turmeric, ground black pepper, coconut oil and honey each morning. This, allegedly, improves resistance to illness.

Whatever, I have the smoothies and turmeric because I like the taste.

Diabetes

Sometime in 1996, a colleague noticed as passed his desk with a fifth or sixth pint, that I was drinking a lot of water. My GP confirmed what he and my wife had anticipated. I had diabetes. My mother was Type 2 diabetic, as were both her mother and her brother, so it was no surprise. For about a month I tried tablets and a diet, with no appreciable effect, except flatulence. The GP then started me on insulin.

I disliked needles so it was pleasant to find that they are so thin that rarely is there any sensation, far less pain.

Vitamins and Minerals

I take huge quantities of vitamins and minerals. The list includes glucosamine & chondroitin, vitamin B complex, inositol (sometimes called vitamin B8), vitamin D3, vitamin E, Omega 3, 6 & 9, a probiotic capsule, garlic extract, magnesium and a zinc tablet. I also take two grams of vitamin C powder dissolved in water, two or three times daily and my turmeric drink each morning.

I have seen all functional seizures cease since I started this regime.

Milk

Apart from the warm third pint bottles at school, I have always loved milk.

In Sofia, Bulgaria on the last day of a project for the national Telecom Company, just before Christmas, a shindig was thrown by the employees. I joined after it had been on for some hours, in a room where the air was blue with cigarette smoke. There was great excitement at having finished a project not only on time but to budget, something thought impossible for the BTC.

I was offered a choice of raki or some home-made red wine. I declined both. I also refused some salami the sight of which made my stomach turn cartwheels.

Bulgaria is heavily carnivorous, and it was difficult to find anything a veggie would eat, though *shopska* salad, hummus and ice-cold cucumber soup are local dishes, so I never went hungry, despite limited choices.

The salami was followed by sugary cakes which I couldn't accept because of my diabetes. Desperate to show their hospitality I was asked if I would like a glass of milk. I accepted out of politeness but with no idea of what was to come.

A much-faded Coke bottle, almost full, appeared from a haversack. As it was poured, a stream of lumps flowed into the glass. I had refused other offerings, so I needed to make a good show of enjoying the milk. I needn't have worried. The milk was ice cold (it was minus ten degrees outside) and was the freshest, most delicious, rich, moreish milk I had had in a long time, probably ever. The lumps were cream, and the milk had still been in a cow eight hours before. Over the next hour, unashamedly I finished the two litres, to the delight of my hosts. I was dubbed '*milkman*' on my next assignment in country, the following year.

Wellness and Healthy Activities

As far back as I can remember, I have been active. This served me well. Swimming, surfing, kayaking, walking, occasionally running, cycling very often, sailing too little and other activities were avenues for adventure and development.

The long-term benefits are not imaginary. They are measurable. My heart rate at rest usually hovers around 60 BPM (it was in the low 30's after the Tour de France). My blood pressure rarely exceeds 120/70 and often is below.

Before FND, I was active and physically very engaged. In my forties when in London on business, I would take a five or six mile walk from the City to Hammersmith and my hotel, in preference to the tube.

Ten years on in Sofia, Munich and elsewhere, if feasible, I would walk from the office to my hotel. I would take the stairs rather than a lift. Once, in Nokia's HQ, when I was fifty-something, I lagged by less than a couple of minutes behind my colleagues, who took the lift, up thirty-three storeys. They opened a book on which floor I would have my heart attack.

Now I am just as engaged if a lot less active. This is a fact of life.

Mental Health

Bipolar Disorder

I was always a '*bit enigmatic of mood*' (a euphemism for being '*as mad as a box of frogs*'). Recently a school friend observed that in my teens I could be the life and soul of a party one minute and suicidal in an instant. That was put down either to hormones or '*Robert just being Robert*'.

For the decade after school my moods were balanced, probably as I had few triggers. At least there were no obvious mood swings. I had a course of a Valium in my last year at university, not uncommon among students. It lasted only a couple of weeks.

It was only during my first marriage that my moods swung between depression and intense mental activity, which only later I understood as hypomania or mania. A sudden and deep depression could be triggered by a song, or tune. Billy Joel's 'Pianoman' had this effect ('*drinking a drink they call loneliness, it's better than drinking alone*' was a familiar notion).

After my GP told me that I '*definitely was not manic depressive*' but was '*looking for an excuse for time off work*', I had a year of psychotherapy to address my alleged problem, anger, the most 'excessive' of my 'up' symptoms. By coincidence the therapist was the GP's husband and I wonder if family finances were the root of the misdiagnosis, rather than medical judgement.

About a year later I moved and changed GP. I was diagnosed with manic depression, or bipolar disorder. (The stigma is the same by either name.) It is probable that I have been bipolar, undiagnosed, since my teens.

I spent two periods in a Mental Unit in Worcester in an 'elevated' mood. During the second visit my wife of less than two years told me she didn't want me to return to the family home. The threat was not executed immediately but by two months after discharge I knew I was not welcome in my home, so I packed what I could, and left.

The financial cost to say goodbye (although I left without goodbye being said, ceremony or farewells) was by no means trivial. **But leaving was one of the most correct things I have ever done.**

With few minor exceptions, I have not been aware of a hypomanic or manic episode for 20 years though for over a decade, until about seven years ago, I struggled with varying degrees of clinical depression. I seem to have outlived my diagnosis and I am now off all medication for bipolar, with the encouragement of my mental health team.

Looking back, bipolar cost me a lot of things. The stays b in an unsympathetic and unhelpful mental hospital were the start. Losing my home and most of the contents were next. It also scuppered access to my son after about 1991.

I have lost three good and enjoyable jobs. Never was I derelict or unprofessional, nor under-performing. I probably over-performed to hedge against my bipolar becoming known. Nevertheless, the jobs went.

One employer paid me off on a dubious claim that my talents no longer were relevant. My manager was a friend of my boss when I was diagnosed, years before, so I knew what probably had happened but was never likely to prove a connection. Small minds had been made up. End of story. I took the money and walked.

My last employer isolated me on long-term sick leave for eleven years until I retired in 2017.

In common with many people suffering disabling conditions, friends and neighbours do not want to know, though there have been a few exceptions. I know how distressing it is to be the only family in a small, closely grouped hamlet of less than five families, not to be invited to a midsummer's night party and, with our windows open, to hear the laughter from the goings-on next door.

Nearer to home, one of my in-laws once asked my wife if '*Robert is still mad?*' It was not an isolated incident. The son of my father's best man and closest friend for eighty years, suffered from schizophrenia. My father was ashamed of my diagnosis and never even told him I was bipolar.

I am no longer ashamed of my diagnosis, nor coy in admitting it. I regret that bipolar is a convenient weapon, an insult and is painful and damaging when used. The stigma attached to any mental illness is insidious and actions and reactions hurt and damage deeply.

Cancer, the Big C

In September 2005 this part of the story almost began. '*Almost began*' as it nearly went unnoticed and could have been quite different.

I became aware of a lump the size of a duck's egg, on my neck and below my jaw. I assumed it would go away by itself. It did not, so as my usual doctor was on leave, I saw a locum. He assured me that it was probably nothing but put me on antibiotics as a precaution. In retrospect, it was like the observation of Captain Arthur Smith of the Titanic, about there being '*no icebergs this far south at this time of year*'. My wife wasn't concerned either, or she kept it to herself.

Over Christmas I saw my regular GP about something and in passing I mentioned the lump. She felt my neck and referred me to the top '*lumps on the neck*' guy in one of Dublin's hospitals. It took only a fortnight to receive an appointment, yet I still wasn't worried as the lump wasn't painful, nor had altered size, texture, colour, or shape.

In the clinic, after a superficial examination, there were X-rays, an ultrasound, and an MRI scan. There was a follow up appointment a couple of weeks later when a pathologist took a sample of fluid from the lump. The sample was examined, and I was invited to another appointment some weeks away.

At home, the same evening the phone rang. *"Could you come to the clinic next Wednesday? It will save having to wait for the results to come in the post".*

Oh yes, this has a tail, squeaks, and eats cheese. Less than four hours ago it was OK to have a follow-up in two or three weeks. Now it was three working days. We both knew that the lump was not to be ignored, nor was likely to go away by itself.

St David's Day and I was in an excellent mood. At the clinic we met a Doctor and an Oncology specialist nurse manager. The latter was a plot spoiler. They both were graver and more serious than I felt inclined to be.

The Doctor confirmed my diagnosis, a malignant tumour in the lymph nodes in my neck, a *metastatic squamous cell carcinoma*. The analysis showed it was a secondary cancer in my neck with a primary and possibly other secondaries elsewhere. The choice of treatment was a combination of surgery followed by radio- or chemotherapy, or palliative care. I did not fancy the last one.

It doesn't matter who you are, who you know, what you did or how much money you have; if Big C comes a-looking, it will find you! On the other hand, what you do after it finds you is vital. I think it is fair that my reaction was to see it as little more than a temporary setback, an interruption of a summer's cycling. I had every confidence that it was curable, and I could cope with it. A belief that failure was not an option.

From the start I had an upbeat approach. Positive Mental Attitude and my appalling and incorrigible sense of humour. I was strong, I was determined, and I was not afraid.

After my operation the surgical team told my wife that they thought, without surgery, I had only about two weeks to live. I later found out that the prospect of surviving over five years after any mouth cancer is less than twenty percent. Then again, in WW2, space on US aircraft carriers was at a premium and it was proposed to remove six or more feet from the fuselage of the aircraft. They tried it and it worked. Someone remarked that the laws of aerodynamics it shouldn't have been able to fly. The riposte was *"Neither should the Bumble Bee but nobody told the Bumble Bee"*.

No-one told my cancer the prognosis.

Surgery and the prognosis

On the day of surgery, I was calm and relaxed although wanting it to be over and done. The operation was a big one, with several surgeons in attendance, a perverse sort of flattery. I came to in a recovery room about seven hours after I went under. The procedure was longer than anticipated due to the unexpected size and configuration of the growth. They had removed all 23 lymph glands from the right side of my neck, seven of these had cancerous cells. I also lost a jugular artery, a section of the base of the tongue and a muscle section from top shoulder to middle chest.

I needed about forty metal staples which gave my throat the appearance of having a zip.

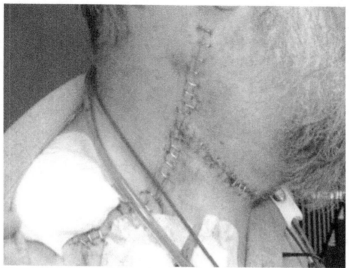

You can't see from this angle where the bolt was.

By late evening, a drain in my neck was seeping more fluid than was healthy and there was a concern that my airway would be compromised. I was returned to theatre to cure the bleed. After, I felt fresh and not nauseous, unlike the first time when I threw up over two nurses and my wife. I never made it out of the recovery room as the drain still was getting more fluid than was acceptable and they operated a third time.

I became aware of a bright white light directly in front of me. My immediate thought was *'Oh bugger, this is IT'. I am going towards the light'*. I felt no fear just irrational contentment, and warmth. Then I saw the faces of the surgical team looking at me. I had woken up on the operating table, something confirmed by one of the nurses and by the anaesthetist (who also remembered my reaction: *"This is surreal. Anyone know any dirty jokes?"*).

It was a week before I was told that the primary was near my tonsils, or where they used to be. Radiotherapy was the next step, and the prognosis was good. When explained that the cancer was in metastatic squamous cells I responded to the doctor, *"You mean cancer cells that can't bear the sight of blood?"* This drew a blank, so I explained *"Metastatic squeamish cell carcinoma...?"* at which she groaned, but I hope that she dined out on the tale.

Radiotherapy and Chemotherapy

For radiotherapy I had a full head mask, less attractive than the one in Phantom of the Opera, to clamp me to the treatment table. Before the first of my thirty-nine sessions, I asked *"Have you got enough shillings for the meter?"* but my audience was too young to remember either coin-fed meters or shillings. After this session I felt I was on my way to wellness and was a 'proper' cancer patient.

My chemo, over seven weeks provided a relief from the ward. For each session, back in Beaumont, I was settled in a comfortable chair and received an infusion of saline to hydrate me. Then the chemo of choice was administered. It came in opaque bags, marked with dire warnings. The staff wore gloves and full PPE and treated the liquid with extreme care and respect. Infusion took between one and four hours, then more saline was infused. It meant long and wearisome days.

Chemotherapy is said to be like sea sickness having two phases: *'Can it kill me?'* and *'Please can it kill me?'*. However, I suffered no large side effects, such as sickness and nausea. (I had taken the precaution of ticking the 'No sickness' and 'No nausea' boxes when admitted.) The worst part was boredom. I soon tired of reading, and I would lapse into a semi-vegetative state, dribbling and playing with my fingers and mouth. I took a laptop intending to write a great twenty-first century smutty novel. I also tried to read a biography of Lawrence of Arabia but later I reverted to the Narnia Chronicles then to the *Beano* and the *Dandy*. Often, I just slept.

Lessons from Health and Wellness

Unhealth and the antidotes

Try not to dwell on your symptoms as indicators of a disability, although to others they may seem to be. Instead, regard them as areas where you may have a reduced scale of ability and then constantly look to find or develop ways around the shortcomings.

Be determined and independent. I am this to the point of being stubborn and with a tendency for perfection this helps me to apply the philosophy. Others call it OCD, or evidence of my being autistic or having Asperger's. I call it normal, and I live with it.

Be mildly obsessive about some things, even if they seem trivial. One of my obsessions is for objects not to be moved from where I leave them. With FND this is more acute as if, for example, when I try and prepare breakfast, I find that the box of cereal is not where it I left it, this wastes time and having to look for it depletes a limited supply of energy.

I find myself weary to the point of collapse by mid evening, so having to waste time searching for something I thought I knew where it was, is annoying. It is not OCD.

Be ready to learn to change the basics, even your lifestyle and habits, your body tells you to do this. Listen to your inner voice. Sometimes to ignore it will bring grim consequences.

Abstinence is a personal choice, sometimes very personal. Absent essentials like water, food, and air, you can give up anything if you want. It helps to have an incentive, preferably a strong one, such as continuing to live, breathe or maintain a decent standard of living and health.

Even something that looks awful may bring a manifest of wonderful surprises. Yes, even FND.

Mental Health

Maintaining a Positive Mental Attitude is essential to fight any illness, holding hands with your faith and following the treatment recommended by your medical team.

However well prepared you think you are you may discover for yourself that stigma hurts, that stigma is unnecessary, that stigma is unkind, and that stigma is always stigma.

However, even with a chronic or disabling condition you may still achieve great things. Clive of India, Disraeli, Hemmingway and many others succeeded despite being bipolar. It is a choice, your choice, not an alternative. Remember the bumblebee?

This is what you can do. Fly despite difficulty or the circumstances and despite what '*they*' might say. Strive to reach beyond your grasp. Look and plan beyond your immediate horizon. Never let anyone and particularly not your own inner voice persuade you that you cannot! Then use each and every activity, obstacle or challenge as a form of therapy.

Reflection.

Not every illness or disability is visible.

There's an old tale about a man who goes to a doctor and says he's depressed, that life seems harsh and cruel, that he feels alone in a threatening world where what lies ahead is vague and uncertain.

The doctor says, "Treatment is simple. The great clown Pagliacci is in town tonight. He cheers up everyone who sees him. Go to the show. That is certain to pick you up."

The man bursts into tears and cries out "But doctor, I am Pagliacci."

Outdoor Activities

Of all the outdoor activities I have enjoyed, cycling, and sailing have brought the most profound experiences, so I will not dwell on others.

Cycling

I learned to ride a bike when I was eight or nine on a neighbour's bike, in the back streets behind our house. Home was adjacent to a fast and dangerous curve, and I was not allowed to have my own bike. The prohibition lasted until I went to university and, as a concession for not being supplied with a car, I 'inherited' my father's sit up and beg, wartime bike, complete with 25-year-old war issue tyres and almost wholly ineffective rod brakes.

It was fun while it lasted, despite Bath University being on the top of one of the City's hills and the weekly shopping expedition, was to town, at the bottom. I never managed to ride all the way up Bathwick Hill, despite several attempts.

The bicycling student era paused in my second year as I had a Lambretta scooter, barely powerful enough to climb the hill and with two up, nearly impossible. It was a fine means of transport and provided some fun when I took it (with camping kit, girlfriend and surfboard) to Croyde Bay in North Devon coast and later back to Swansea.

In my final year I had my first car, an aging maroon Volkswagen Beetle. I was proud of the car, having worked all summer, doing nights in a pork pie factory in Wiltshire to buy it. My father dismissed it as '*an old banger*', but such casual criticism did not concern me. It was, after all, my first car.

Skewjack Surf Village, Cornwall, 1974, after finals.

The beloved old war horse fell to pieces shortly after I graduated. In London, I had no need for a car as the underground or a bus was more convenient. This lasted until a summer job in a brewery in Mortlake. An unsociably early start and two buses each way, prompted my buying another old black bike, and. This stirred my enduring love of cycling.

London years, *au vélo*

A car was always impractical, inconvenient and beyond my budget, so unless it was a 'posh frock' do, I relied on my bike. In summer 1978, on a 'racing' bike to which I had graduated, on Lower Richmond Road in Putney, I nearly met my end when a car turned across in front of me. We collided, sending me, bike and all, flying over the bonnet to land head-first on the pavement. This wrote off the bike and put me in hospital with an ugly gash across my forehead, a cut on the bridge of my nose and a chipped tooth. The wounds healed, the tooth was replaced with a crown and in time the scar faded. Nevertheless, I was shaken, for a while.

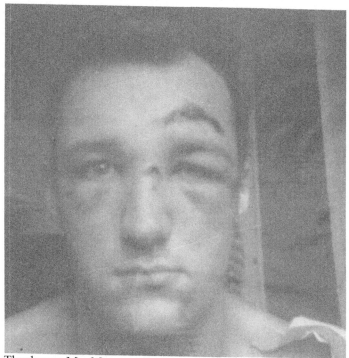

Thank you, Mrs Margaret Foxton, your Vauxhall Viva and Lower Richmond Road, Putney.

This did not deter me from cycling, although it was a year before I bought a new bike. In 1979 I toured Youth Hostels in the Cotswolds and east Wales with my then girlfriend. My first cycling tour.

I returned to work in Smithfield, the other side of London from Fulham where I lived and felt that the Underground was no match for cycling the journey. I started what then was unfashionable - commuting by bike. My route meant negotiating Marble Arch and Oxford Street, twice daily, but included a pleasant ride across Hyde Park.

The next year with the same companion as on the Cotswold tour, I cycled from John O'Groats to Land's End. It was memorable and woke my interest in longer distance cycling, but it sounded the death knell for the relationship.

A year on and I discovered 'randonneur' events. These are timed rides, subject to minimum and maximum speeds. Shortest events are 200 km, ridden as an individual. These were no great challenge, save for an unforgettable 200, in Dorset in the snow when I froze my bum off.

The company on these rides usually was excellent. There is no class on randonneurs. You are cyclists, Period. I had the company of, among others, a solicitor, a vet who specialised in artificial insemination, a painter and decorator, a London Transport tube driver and the warden of the Youth Hostel in Salisbury.

After getting my 'Brevet' Card stamped, Surrey Hills Grimpeur (climbing) 100km, 1981. I finished third fastest, despite never claiming any prowess as a climber. I guess that I had a good day's legs.

I progressed to 300 km rides, although I did not take to these as they started at 2 a.m. and meant riding through the night and most of the next day. The distance was less a problem than getting to the start in time and having adequate rest before and during the event.

After this I rode a string of 400 km rides and then a couple of 600s, the Windsor-Chester-Windsor and the Caen 600 km, in Normandy. These were a week apart. After the W-C-W, I cycled to work on Monday to Thursday, then took an overnight ferry to Cherbourg, riding 150 km to Caen on Friday, the day before the second event. I returned from France two days and 600 km later, on the Sunday night ferry to Portsmouth and was at my desk in Smithfield at 9 am on the Monday morning to put in a full day's work. That was after riding 1,400 km in 9 days. If I wasn't fit, I certainly was resilient.

I packed in on one 400, when I realised that I had ridden the same route a month before and knew that food at the turn was a rather nasty greasy spoon chippy. Instead, I took up a standing invitation to visit a girlfriend somewhere close to the route. Aside from this, my sole failure was the 1000 km Vendôme to Brest and back. Two of us, of four starters, realised we were further behind time than was feasible to make up, so after about 350 kms we turned back. Not memorable save for spending a night under a tree, on the return leg.

That was my first full season.

Tour de France Randonnée

Far and away at the top of my '*palmares*' (achievements) came in September 1982, with the Tour de France Randonnée.

How often in the scheme of things does an adventure start with a chance remark? My epic was launched in a routine call to a friend. I had taken delivery of a new bike and had a vague idea of riding across France to Andorra, where I had never there. Mick suggested that the Tour de France would probably be more enjoyable.

The Tour de France Randonnée is not the race of the same name, nor does it follow the race route. It was and probably still is the longest organised tourist cycling event in the world. It follows the borders of France, is about 2,000 to 3,000 km further than the race and in a similar number of days, albeit at a slower pace and over more hours a day. You may start and finish anywhere on the route and go clockwise or anticlockwise. These are your choices. The only stipulations are that your progress is certified in a *Brevet de Route* and your maximum time must not exceed thirty days. My *grand boucle* began and ended in Calais, and I took just over 25 days, covering a tad over 4,900 km.

From Calais I went North then East on the French side of the Belgium/Germany border, through the Alsace to Geneva. From there it was South through the Alps to Nice, 560 mountainous kilometres in three days, including several major Cols including the Col de la Bonette, the highest pass in the Alps. Then three days in baking heat along the Corniche to Perpignan. On the last day on this section my companion packed in and flew home as he had heard that his father was dangerously ill. I had a choice, to give up and go, or to carry on alone. I chose the latter, never thinking that, if I succeeded, I would be the first Brit to complete the ride.

After Perpignan it was west to the Atlantic over some of the biggest climbs in the Pyrenees, then a succession of routine 200 km days to return to the start.

The last day, my 26th day, started at Abbeville on the Somme. It was raining at 06:30 and I needed my rain jacket. It was slow and weary progress. At Boulogne my fatigue made me consider giving up, after 4870 km with 30 to go, the only time I considered abandoning.

Outside Calais, I paused at the top of the hill overlooking the town, tidied up the bike and put away my rain jacket. Then the last few kms to the end in the low ratio gear I had used to crawl to the summit. The road rolled down and I worked up through the gears. As the town sign drew into sight, I shifted into top gear and in Tour de France style, I rose from the saddle and sprinted wildly for the line. Just short of 'Calais' I sat back and crossed the line with my hands in the air in a traditional racing salute.

No-one witnessed the moment! That is how it should be. The ride was mine, mine alone and of no relevance to anyone else.

My participant's bike plaque, finishers' lapel badge and the gold medal. Just plastic and metal memories, somewhere in a drawer.

I never rode another Randonnée. I had sated my appetite for miles, though from time to time I considered trying to go anticlockwise. There's still a spark, maybe on a trike.

Sailing and yachts

In my teens I learned to sail in a Mirror dinghy my father had made from a kit. The family graduated to a GRP Enterprise dinghy, rather inclined to roll on wet grass but fun to sail in a breeze, if you enjoy a sudden cold bath and the taste of sea water.

Big boys' toys

I learned a few things about sailing and after some years I graduated to big boys' toys. My first command was a 26-foot sloop called Brandy Cove which I chartered and with three others, my sister Juliet, a colleague, Guy and his wife. We sailed from Swansea to Milford Haven and back, pausing overnight, each way in Tenby's little harbour. I was Skipper of the largest boat in the harbour!

I also had a lot of adventures in Goldilocks, my father's second 'real' boat, though always as crew, cook, navigator or chief mackerel catcher. Never as skipper, unthinkable to my father.

Over the years I crewed friends' boats across the English Channel including a swift crossing in the forefront of a hurricane. I also navigated a delivery trip from the Solent to Plymouth, an arduous 36-hour non-stop voyage, made more adventurous (difficult, dangerous) by a very inexperienced and unprepared skipper/owner. I chalked it down to 'experience'.

Rojan was my own first boat. An Elizabethan 31 (foot) masthead sloop with a deep keel. She was no ocean greyhound, but was stable and sea kindly, a forgiving ship. I kept her in Portsmouth Harbour and pottered about on the Solent before moving her to Penarth, near Cardiff. She was my sanctuary when my first marriage was disintegrating.

On Rojan, single handed, off Penarth.

My second and last yacht was *Goosewing II*, a Westerly 33-foot ketch. With two masts she was beautifully balanced and easy to sail, even single handed, a steady, comfortable but not speedy boat.

Really big boats

I sailed on Sir Winston Churchill, the Sail Training Association's 130-foot tops'l schooner, as a humble trainee, in November 1980. I also sailed on her sister ship, the Malcolm Miller. I had over a dozen trips on the schooners as cook's mate, bosun's mate, watch leader and watch officer and my last and least favourite trip was the 1985 Tall Ship's Race. I was disillusioned with the STA and the race was a bad experience due to various factors. I decided that enough was enough. I have not missed the schooners, nor regretted my decision.

Sometimes, you try to sleep, – 'try' being the operative word.

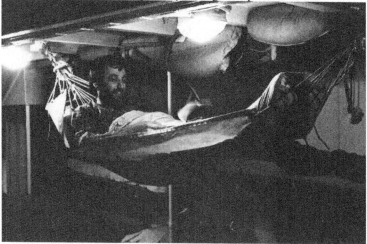

I was introduced to Royalist, the Sea Cadet Corps' 80-foot brig, by a girl I had met on the Churchill. Unfortunately, between my applying for the cruise and joining the ship, the relationship unilaterally had been terminated. This was a shock, and the inevitable tension was unpleasant, made worse as she refused to speak to me, not even to explain why she had distanced herself. Emotionally her ship had sailed without me. I was confused and bewildered for the whole week. It was particularly complicated as we were co-leaders of a watch and had to communicate.

After the cruise I never saw nor spoke to her again, though I sailed on Royalist twice more, most enjoyably.

Yachtmaster

Between 1984 and 1985 I took RYA shore-based courses for Competent Crew, Day Skipper and Yachtmaster itself. I had the experience and sea miles for Competent Crew and Day Skipper from serving on the Churchill, Miller and Royalist. In 1986, a cruel and public observation by my father when we were waiting for the lock gates to open in Swansea Marina, spurred me to go further. I had suggested a different way to do something. He remarked, loud enough to be heard clearly by the couple of dozen onlookers, who laughed, was *"Oh. so, the boy has read a book!"* This was my incentive. I took a refresher course and then the practical exam, the most enjoyable day that I ever spent under sail. Everything went right and I qualified as a RYA/DTI Yachtmaster.

CERTIFICATE OF COMPETENCE

AS

YACHTMASTER OFFSHORE

No. 06599

To Mr R Wilson-Thomas

WHEREAS you have been examined to standards approved by the Department of Transport (Marine Directorate) and found duly qualified as a Yachtmaster Offshore the Royal Yachting Association hereby grant you this Certificate of Competence

Date of issue
12-09-86

Approved on behalf of RYA/DTP
Yachtmaster Qualifications Panel

My father, with many times my experience in small boats, twice tried and twice failed his Yachtmaster practical. Then he gave up. Some months after his second failure he was bemoaning his failures. I mentioned, probably after a snipe at my sailing ability that I had passed. Revenge is a dish best served cold, though I knew I had hurt him, deeply, something that he tried, but failed, to hide.

In meant that ever after, all questions about any sailing topic accompanied with a snide *"What does 'the Yachtmaster' think?"*.

Lessons from Outdoor Activities

Cycling

I learned from '*ancients*' in France to "*Eat before you are hungry, drink before you are thirsty and rest before you are tired.*" This is sound advice in whatever you are engaged. I have found it particularly relevant with survival with FND.

With this you may find you can go further, much further than you think. Do not dwell on the total distance, nor the destination or goal. Concentrate on the next metre, kilometre, rest of the day. Every turn of the pedals makes progress. It is a matter of taking one turn of the pedals, or one foot in front of another.

You do whatever you do for yourself, not for transitory glory or the tuppence worth of tin in a medal.

Fellow FND sufferers will understand and appreciate the effort you make, even if a sceptical and critical majority don't recognise what you put in.

If in doubt, just go there, do that.

Sailing and yachts

The theory is the same, irrespective of the size of the boat. One hand for yourself, one hand for the ship, the origin of why a sailor is called a 'hand'. When my wife was in hospital for three weeks it was how, with my difficulty standing, I learned to cook. One hand holding on, the other stirring or jiggling a frying pan.

Take one watch at a time and remember that all storms blow over, eventually. It may be uncomfortable, but is it unsafe?

Seasickness has two phases. "*Can it kill me?*" and "*Please can it kill me?*". Somewhat familiar questions for FND sufferers.

Night vision is best served by using peripheral vision, looking without staring in one place. In FND terms it means not staring at a problem or obstacle for too long, as you will get polarised and may miss a simple but less obvious solution.

Life with the deck (floor) sloping at 40 degrees and moving about wildly is still life. It may be uncomfortable and inconvenient, perhaps risky, or dangerous at times, but it is still life. It means adapting to a new normal. Furniture surfing when you cannot find your feet is like moving about a deck with a running sea, in a gale.

Plan your next move, your hand hold or safe place, and the one after that and enjoy the ride!

Sex, Drugs and Rock and Roll

I feel that I should cover this, as not all my activities were entirely healthy. Fun perhaps, but dubiously 'healthy'.

Rude introduction

Among my earliest memories was an episode that still haunts me.

When I was 6 or 7 years old, maybe even younger, two men tried to groom me.

The family was on holiday, in a caravan above a bay. I was 'befriended' by the two 'lads' and felt pleased to be paid some attention. With my parents' consent, they walked with me up the hill to a van in the field next to ours and I was invited inside. The curtains were drawn as, they said, a neighbour was always coming round to borrow things and she was a nuisance. This sounded reasonable, even to a child.

I remember exactly what I was wearing (a blue flannel bathing costume with a white felt appliqué of a cowboy chasing some Red Indians). I recall distinctly the most minute of details of what happened. Like the invitations to take off my costume, saying it was normal. Their overtures felt wrong, I resisted and after about an hour I was allowed to leave. It was probably a narrow escape, though from what is conjecture.

I told my father about the incident. He did nothing, even when I pointed out the lads in the camp shop the next morning.

This episode is fresh even now, 60 years later and shows the impact it had. I want no-one to have a similar experience to cloud their life.

Sex

After the caravan incident, my life resumed its asexual existence and had a decade of quiet. There was some basic sex education at primary school, but it was clouded in animals, birds, and bees. A connection with human activity was not made. My father took me aside when I was 13 and vividly described that. I spent the next month looking at adults thinking 'You really do *that?*'

These thoughts passed. By sixteen or seventeen I knew there were ways to enjoy life other than trudging up mountains in the rain and surfing all year round. From the coarse brags of other lads, it seems that the joy of sex had been discovered earlier for some than for others, or for me.

From my first fumbling in the dark in the back rows of the cinema, I enjoyed mixed and patchy fortunes in most of my relationships.

My first girlfriend, when I was 17, I met at a theatre in Swansea. It was '*one price all seats*' on Monday's performance in the repertory season. With a couple of friends, I went each week for several years.

I went out with R for about four months and then she finished the relationship abruptly and for no apparent reason, well, none that was apparent to me. I was sweet on her, but never said anything. An irony is that some years later I introduced her to her future husband, but was not invited to the wedding, probably as I had been badly behaved with a bridesmaid at the engagement party.

After a string of juvenile relationships, all casual, I severed all romantic links and relationships when I went to university.

In the three years at Bath I tried, unsuccessfully to date widely, but had two steady girlfriends. The first was assertive, rather cool and distant. The other was the opposite. Consensual, adventurous, and warm. I torpedoed that after I moved to London, and she stayed in Bath to complete her final year. She objected to my having a new paramour. Who could blame her? Whilst the Neil Young song goes

"*If you can't be with the one you love, love the one you're with*", my decision to do this I came to regret, quite deeply.

In London there was a succession of partners, not always monogamous or sequential, none lasting too long nor involving significant emotional attachment.

Yes, typical testosterone driven male behaviour.

Drugs

I had flirted with solvents as a teenager in the 1970s, but in University I discovered the joys of marijuana. Cannabis was pure, cheap (even compared to beer at Student Bar prices), and available.

The experience of sharing a joint in a dimly lit hall of residence bedroom, with incense and usually some vague and mystic music, was enjoyable and gave me insights and a euphoria I had never known. I stopped smoking when I began dating a pharmacy student whose career would have come to an end if I had been busted.

I never dropped acid, nor tried speed. Neither interests me.

By a twist of fate, my next association with drugs was six years later in my first pupillage. In 1977 we defended, successfully, the first person in the UK to be charged with possession of liberty cap, or 'magic' mushrooms, *psilocybe semilanceata*. In mid-2021, magic mushrooms resurfaced when I heard about an Australian researcher doing clinical trials on the use of psilocybin-assisted psychotherapy to treat patients with certain FND symptoms.

Rock and roll (and other influences)

I discovered rock music in my teens, on the recommendation of a Franciscan friar Brother Paul, who had an eclectic taste in music. He also introduced me to folk music.

Through surfing, another Paul, a close friend I still talk with, I heard and fell in love with Crosby Stills, Nash & Young. *Teach your Children* (the original, with Gerry Garcia of Grateful Dead, on slide guitar) is my favourite track of any era, for the lyrics and the harmonies. I tried and failed to teach my parents anything.

Aside from a broad appreciation of romantic classical music, I listen mostly to artists of the Woodstock era, and those who have been influenced by them. Folk music is a regular feature. I stopped playing my guitars and ceased singing in public a few years back.

To my pride, in the early 1990s, I played acoustic guitar on a record made by the retro rock and roll teddy boy group, Showaddawaddy. You leap back, astonished and exclaim *"What, you made a record with Showaddawaddy?"*

Yes, I did, I really did, though there is a subtle twist.

They (we) broke the Guinness Book of World Records for the most guitarists playing the same song at the same time. It was in a gym in Hereford. There were 136 electric guitars, all with amplifiers turned to maximum, frantically trying to outdo each other, plus my mate Dave Lu and myself on our acoustic guitars.

We played a solid 40 minutes of '*Shake Rattle and Roll*' and the record was ours.

I was partially deaf for the next three days.

Lessons from Sex, Drugs and Rock and Roll

I could say not to be afraid of experimenting or trying something new, but with the caveat that I do not advocate the use of illegal substances. Otherwise, an open mind is essential to progress.

In time, I believe medicinal marijuana will become sanctioned and adopted as a therapy for some symptoms of FND. As of now, there is a little scientific proof about it, though plenty of anecdotal evidence. The latter does not count with professionals. They are loath to adopt what limited access there is to medicinal marijuana, nor will until there has been significant research. That may be years away, although I know one professional, in the UK who is monitoring a trial and already talks about '*promising results*'.

Similarly, psychiatric, or physiotherapeutic intervention have been floated as a possible intervention to treat FND symptoms. Some may be effective though the returns are not immediately discernible.

I believe in challenging, changing and exploring dietary regimes, much of which is based on habit, and the use of exercise and a robust approach to vitamins and other natural supplements.

Marriage, love and thereafter

First complete and utter disaster

I met my first wife at a party, in my home on my birthday. A friend asked if she could bring someone who needed a good night out. We hit it off and were married ten months later. A colossal mistake. I knew it then but chose to ignore my hunches to regret it later.

During the marriage my moods, possibly coincidentally, began to swing between sudden and acute depression and periods of intensity. I had psychotherapy after my GP ruled out manic depression. Only later was I diagnosed with bipolar disorder.

During the second of two periods in a Mental Unit in Worcester, my wife told me that she did not want me to return to the family home. No discussion, just I don't want you home. Two months on it was clear I was not welcome. I had outlived my usefulness and I left.

The cost to say goodbye was appreciable but psychologically and emotionally, leaving was the most correct thing I have ever done.

I was prevented from seeing my son. I would arrive to find he was '*unwell*' or '*playing elsewhere with a friend*' or just '*didn't want to see me*' or there was some other reason. For one birthday I agreed to come to his party. When I rang in the morning to confirm the time, I was told that it had been moved to the previous Saturday. This was just cruel. It hurt me and probably disappointed my son. I saw that my wife held all the cards and I ceased to visit. It was too frustrating and painful.

After a few years I applied to the Court to try and regain contact. My ex-wife (who I had not seen for over 4 years) opened her case against access by claiming that I was '*dangerously mentally ill*' and '*unsafe to be with children*'. Both statements were without foundation nor proof. They were pounced on by the court and without seeking evidence or my response, access was granted at a centre a further 30 miles distant from where I lived (making a hundred-and forty-mile round trip for an hour's visitation) and always was to be with supervision. A further condition was that my '*ex*' had to agree to each visit. Her track record meant the likelihood of her both agreeing to a visit and then turning up with my son was so remote that contact would be minimal, or probably nil.

I knew it was against my son's interests to make him ammunition in a war between his parents. I never again saw him after 1991.

Second marriage

Remarriage has been described as "*The triumph of hope over experience*". Oscar Wilde massaged this into "*Marriage is the triumph of imagination over intelligence. Second marriage is the triumph of hope over experience.*"

Marion and I married, in Cortona, Tuscany, Italy in September 2002.

Reality

Since FND visited me, I found an incongruity between the how my symptoms show and both how they are received by others. So-called 'friends' and neighbours, and even my family evaporated swiftly. A couple of my neighbours have decided to ignore and to shun us.

These were distressing when I realised what was happening, but their impact has lessened with time.

Lessons from Marriage and love

You have to kiss a lot of frogs before you find your princess.

I spent a lot of time philandering with Miss Right Now, most pleasurably, before I thought that I had found my Miss Right. Even then I was mistaken, or more accurately taken in and taken. Then the future Mrs Right appeared.

Two quotations:

"Tis better to have loved and lost than never to have loved at all."
Alfred, Lord Tennyson (In Memoriam A.H.H.)

More positively, I can say no better than to quote Dylan Thomas.

"Though lovers be lost, love shall not ...."
(And Death shall have no Dominion)

Travelling

Are we there, yet, Mum?

Flying

Travelling and flying could occupy a book by themselves. At last count I had made more than 450 flights, in the course of about 240 or so overseas jaunts. Everything from a Cessna (my only parachute jump) to Concorde (a last-minute upgrade after I missed an earlier flight to New York), plus many aircraft in between, in, variously economy, business and first class.

Most were enjoyable, many, were routine and tedious and on business were spent working or reading. Not a few journeys were uncomfortable.

A couple were decidedly dangerous.

Frequency

Over a half a century, despite about two decades when I made few overseas trips, I went abroad over two hundred times, the majority in the periods 1997 to 2000 and 2001 to 2005. It was not uncommon to have two overseas visits in a week, say Warsaw on Monday and Tuesday, Wednesday in the office and Thursday and Friday in Bucharest.

After my first couple of business trips, I realised that they were not the beano that people who do not travel on business, think them. They are not a free ride around the world, on expenses, eating, drinking and seeing the sights at someone else's cost. It frequently comes down to a flight, a taxi, a hotel, an office, repeating the last two until the trip comes to an end, one way or another, then reversing direction to return home. Trips are not measured by enjoyment but in increments of discomfort and intensity of the activity whilst *'there'*. Such travel and periods of intense activity, though perversely enjoyable, carries a cost

You can tell from the weariness in my face the toll that quarter end exacted. This was eight days after Q2 2002, and on the morning ferry to Holyhead, *en route* to Italy to get married.

Occasionally, scheduling meant a couple of days in a nice location. Minsk is not in this category, though Venice, Melbourne, New York or San Francisco or most European capitals could be. The routine and working stopovers, eating room service and word-mongering until the early hours, was what I was paid for. Days and sometimes weeks away from home, far outnumbered an occasional jolly.

In general, I was fortunate that I never suffered with jetlag, save for a notable occasion after being in Hong Kong (GMT +8 hours) one week and after a few days at home, I flew to Colorado (GMT -8 hours). I was shattered when I arrived, early evening local time and was ready to crash out. The hotel had a fax for me, from a client in Hong Kong. She insisted that a document be amended before I went to sleep, so she didn't lose the rest of her business day.

The 16-hour time difference was worsened by my lack of sleep and that I had worked on the flight from London. I was out of excuses and tiredness was not acceptable. I was starting to hallucinate by 02:00 and I hit the hay. This was around 10am and 6pm the following day, my body time and I woke after only two hours.

When going West, I lengthened my day. The other way with an evening departure and an overnight flight, I tried to wake just before I was due to land, or for breakfast. I would set my watch (and stomach) to the destination time, drank plenty of water and ate when my watch told me to. Problems then were little ones.

Later, needing insulin, my routine took care and planning. On long flights, say to the far coast of the USA or to Brazil or Australia, I predicted when I would eat, took my insulin and ate accordingly. To San Francisco I would have four meals on the outward day but only two on the return leg. On shorter trips, in Europe, even with a transfer, I could ignore the time and inject when I was about to eat.

Travelling Business Class is much better than in economy. You get a decent sized seat, substantially more leg room and space to work. The food, generally, is good. First Class is nice although, even with yet more space, better food and choice, and concentrated service from cabin crew, it is not that better than Business to warrant the cost of an upgrade.

Concorde was cramped but the food was excellent, and it had the major benefit of being very, very fast.

Sarajevo and my worst experience

In 1996, on my way to Sarajevo for the SFOR assignment, I had the worst experience flying, apart from crashing.

Sarajevo is in a basin with mountains on three sides, notorious for cross winds, air pockets and down drafts, a combination for a wild ride. As we left our cruising altitude, we hit an air pocket. For fifteen or twenty seconds we were in freefall. The door to the cockpit flew open and the pilot was frantically pushing the stick from one side to another, desperate to regain control. Locker doors opened and spewed their contents into the cabin. There was screaming and muttered prayers. My most terrifying moment ever.

Fortunately, the pilot regained control and we landed in Sarajevo a bit shaken and stirred. As we crossed the perimeter, a hush descended over the aircraft, other than the continuing rattle of rosary beads. At the last moment the 'plane lifted slightly then touched down softly and gently and as sweetly as though landing on a bed of feathers.

A Lufthansa pilot in the plane after us made three attempts to land. Then he aborted and flew back to Zagreb, telling one of my colleagues on the flight that it was the worst conditions he had encountered in thirty years.

Later, I learned that to the right of the runway was an active minefield. to the left the remains of a village not cleared of anti-personnel mines. Ahead and to each side were mountains, so we were unlikely to be able to do a 'go around'.

With that I lost my enjoyment of flying, at least temporarily.

Fear and CBT

Over the coming months I was nervous before flights and during them, any jolt, sudden noise or turbulence had me gripping the armrests, eyes shut and praying for the ordeal to end. Most passengers probably didn't notice anything, or they did not show it.

The worst flights were out of Sarajevo, when for military restrictions we had to fly at 8,000 feet which meant a half hour white knuckle ride. Worse than this was going from Jo'burg to Gabarone in Botswana in a small propellor plane, we flew through the eye of a thunderstorm.

I had an emergency go-around in Baltimore, when the pilot realised that we were too low to land. There was also an aborted take-off and emergency stop in Zurich when pilot anchored up then did a circuit on the ground before a second attempt at taking off.

My wife, a Senior Occupational Therapist, proposed a method of removing the fear, called *'reframing'*. She told me to imagine I was sitting in a field, watching a TV and a video. Clearly neither was plugged in, so I knew they were imaginary. Then I had to relive the Sarajevo flight in as much detail as I could recall but always with my eyes open. When done I had to 'watch' the video as it rewound and repeat the exercise, several times.

I was unsure if this would help. I was not aware of any change until some weeks later in a patch of turbulence, I realised that I had not looked up from my crossword. I hadn't even noticed the movement and had no reaction, positive or negative.

Reframing was an application of basic psychology. Possibly *'fake it until you make it'* or *'relearn the good habits and override the bad ones'*.

Places

I have travelled all over Europe, most often to France, Germany and Italy, but never to the three Baltic States nor one of the former Yugoslav countries. I worked in about a dozen Central and Eastern European Countries before they left the Soviet bloc. I am proud to have played a small part transitioning thirteen CEECs to EU status.

I also made a couple of visits to Minsk, in Belarus. During one visit I was followed by the KGB, during a walkabout, something I realised after I went through all the many identity papers checks, unchallenged. The Chernobyl nuclear incident had been a few years before and it is possible that my throat cancer was a result of what I may have absorbed on my trips. My manager also went to Minsk but had slightly longer stays. He died of a brain tumour at the time I was recovering from throat cancer.

At Minsk airport, I saw the reality of life for Belarussians. The toilets served both genders and had neither toilet paper nor a wash basin. There were two wire baskets. One held squares of newspaper the other was for used squares of the newspaper. The sewage infrastructure couldn't cope with flushed paper.

My favourite Eastern European destination was Bulgaria, in the 'good old days', before EU influence took its naïve charms. I had two assignments, a year apart and made about 15 visits. There was little choice in shops, but to emphasise who was in charge, the Bulgarian mafia was obvious, with Rolexes, gold chains and vulgar jewellery. They drove state-of-the-art black Saabs with tinted windows and double parked, unchallenged by the police. They always seemed to have a busty, bottled blonde trophy girlfriend, and in restaurants they never had any delay being seated.

Very often after getting into a hotel room the phone would ring and a female would say something like "*Hello, I am a friend of one of your friends. Would you like some company?*". I received such calls in several CEEC countries. In a moment of devilment on one occasion, I told the caller that my manager was in the same hotel and gave her his name and room number. If he had an invitation, he never said. To show how common was the practice, in one hotel in Sofia, each day the bathroom was stocked with a fresh condom.

My first visit to the USA was in 1967 to the scout World Jamboree in Idaho, as a 14-year-old. I loved it. *Everything was big in America.* 15 years later, business took me back and I went many times after. I was in Carmel, California on the morning of 11th September 2001. I saw the best and the worst of America during the weeks that followed. A crazy time, with everyone more than a little hurt and anxious, suspicious of everyone else.

Over one summer I commuted to New York. This was tiring, but some incidentals, like Concorde, made it memorable.

I have been to São Paolo in Brazil and twice to Japan, my spiritual home as it was there that the Buddhism I practice was founded.

I also visited Africa. On one trip, to Botswana I was counsel for Botswana Telecoms in a hearing before the Telecoms Regulator. Mid-assignment I snuck in a safari up country. In Gabarone, capital city of Botswana, I was in a shop, to buy soft drinks, the prices for which was prohibitive in the hotel, and I refused to pay them. I realised I had was an object of scrutiny from other shoppers. It dawned that I was the only white face in the shop. This made me realise a little how, in the 1960s the first Caribbean immigrants to Britain must have felt. At no time did I feel threatened, and it was a positive learning experience.

In Australia, part of a team reorganising the R&D division of the Victorian Gas Company, we were treated to dinner at our contact's home. I forgot to say that I was diabetic and vegetarian, and when his wife asked if anyone had any dietary problems, I mentioned mine and heard a scream from the kitchen.

Lessons from Travelling

Languages

Learn essential words wherever you go. The words for '*Hello*', '*Please*' and '*Thank you*'. '*Can you help me?*' in the local language are useful. If all else fails, ask a teenager for assistance. With the internet, streamed TV and satellite, they are far more likely to understand and speak reasonable English, than their elders.

I had the opposite experience in Thonon on Lake Geneva. I returned to my hotel one afternoon to find four English tourists trying with no success, to explain in English something to *la Patronne*. They turned to me, asked if I could help. I nodded and learned that they had been given one room with two double beds for the four of them. They were two unrelated couples and needed two rooms. I translated this and the patronne said, as they had arrived at the same time, she had assumed that they were travelling together and wanted only one room. Apparently, the French apparently do this sometimes, as I knew from noises I overheard in a cheap hotel in Normandy years earlier.

Fortunately, my French was enough to explain the misunderstanding and to get the mistake corrected. I had a kick when I was told that my English was excellent. I didn't let on.

Learning basic vocabulary applies if your destination is a GP, neurologist, physiotherapist, or another medical professional. Having a basic knowledge of the body, the autonomic nervous system and the nature of FND is more than an advantage. It is a survival tool which helps avoid your being palmed off with an excuse, or worse, a treatment plan or referral to an inappropriate specialist, with little, or no chance of success.

Cultures

Realise cultural differences around the globe. In Bulgaria 'yes' is indicated by shaking the head, not nodding. I found this out the hard way.

Again, it is vital to have a general understanding of the culture of medical professionals. Older GPs tend to be conservative and woefully out of date. They lean towards the '*all in your head*' dismissal of FND. Younger doctors may have heard of the disorder, may be knowledgeable and indeed could be sympathetic.

Other observations

Cherish, embrace, and value differences. People are the principal reason to travel. Do not revisit places where you had a great time as these are unlikely to be repeated. Keep them for memories. Instead, go where you did not enjoy a good time and see if it was you, the company, the moment, or the place.

Do not be envious of other people's 'perks' until you have tried them. Sometimes they have a heavy cost.

Enjoy what there is to enjoy, particularly fresh, local food.

This is as fresh and as local as it gets.

Fresh figs, picked from a tree growing wild by the roadside in Italy.

Cheese! France. The smell would make your hair curl!

Remember the 6P rule - Proper Planning (or Preparation) Prevents Piss Poor Performance. Lists are better than forgetting something essential.

Emotions

I am fortunate as a side effect from FND was an opening of the gates of emotions. This was a shock, as almost all the emotions missing in the previous sixty years hit me at once. Suddenly I had feelings I knew were emotions, but I could neither separate nor identify them individually. Coping with this was difficult at first. Separating guilt and joy, sympathy, empathy, regret and even love, took some months.

A strong sense of empathy developed though this was painful at first. I have learned to embrace it and it helps to drive the direction of my life.

I learned quite recently about the role of emotions and the way in which signals get shuffled around from the various parts of the brain. Little wonder that FND would have such an effect on me. In this case it was a real eye opener.

Lessons from Emotions

Trust your feelings and emotions, they are not your enemies.

Functional Neurological Disorder (FND)

The science, or pseudo-science, Robert's take

FND is a problem with the correct functioning of the autonomic nervous system and how the brain and body send and receive signals. This causes a range of symptoms like gait and balance problems, seizures, weakness, paralysis, fatigue, and chronic pain. FND has multiple causes and can be triggered by physical injury, psychological or other trauma to the brain or to the body. This interrupts proper functioning of the nervous system. The disruption to signals is like letters with a correct label being sent to the wrong address. It has also been compared to a computer where the hardware is sound, but there is a bug in the software.

In recent years, it has been shown that patients with functional movement disorders may exhibit tiny structural white matter abnormalities in critical components of parts of the brain. These abnormalities may be a trait that makes someone more susceptible to illness, to a disease or as having a compensatory response to a disease. This provides some proof that functional movement disorders may have a physical origin

Current best opinion is that FND should not be classed as a mental health disorder nor dismissed as a 'brain condition'. FND is a complex, distinct disorder in which patients suffer from debilitating and often painful neurological symptoms.

The exact cause of FND is unknown. Risk factors like stress, trauma, virus, physical accident or mental health illness are not necessarily the cause of FND. Treatment requires input from a multi-disciplinary team, lead primarily by a specialist neurologist, with some elements able to be addressed by psychiatry.

For most sufferers this is an impossibility. There are not enough neurologists with a knowledge of FND. This is changing, very slowly.

A blanket of general ignorance

FND is misunderstood, misdiagnosed or even its existence denied. Among medical professionals, FND is cloaked in a blanket of general ignorance, despite being the second most frequent reason for an outpatient appointment at a neurology clinic. FND is more prevalent than Multiple Sclerosis and Parkinson's disease combined. Too many GPs have not even heard of FND, nor many A&E units either.

Many medical professions who have heard of FND still cling to an obsolete Freudian concept that '*it is all in your head*' and consign sufferers to the dubious care of psychiatric services. Treatment under a neurologist with the assistance of psychiatry is an improvement. Neuropsychiatrists often are at the cutting edge of research and development, though there are too few about.

FND carries a stigma that can condemn sufferers to wait years for a diagnosis with wasted and expensive medical visits, worsening symptoms, and distress, particularly as symptoms may impair the quality of life, similar and in some respects worse than with Parkinson's' Disease, MS or a stroke.

Currently there is no medication available nor a single known cure for FND although techniques and therapies that may help to relieve some elements of the suffering are always developing. This will accelerate as FND becomes better understood and starts to become more widely recognised. It will start to happen when funding is made available for research.

FND and me

My symptoms and their severity vary from day to day, sometimes even hour to hour or by the minute. They are unpredictable and some can be debilitating. I refuse to accept a label of disabled, preferring to see myself as having limits on my ability and a willingness to try and overcome my limitations.

My most obvious symptom is problems with balance and walking. I have fallen frequently, usually causing just bruising. Occasionally I needed hospital treatment for injuries, and I have been admitted.

Many of my symptoms are common among sufferers with FND and may be summarised as follows.

Gait. (Medically called *ataxia* or Functional Movement Disorder) My walking, even with a stroller or frame, is unsteady and lacks rhythm. My legs can freeze suddenly and without warning. Then gravity can take over.

Balance. I find it difficult to stand unaided for longer than moments. Standing if supported may be done for short periods. Even passing water is edgy. I use furniture or a wall to move and walking independently is possible only with a stroller or someone's support.

Occasionally I have managed to walk independently, slowly and tentatively but only about ten or so steps. This is a rare occurrence. I cannot do this if carrying anything, even a small object such as a coffee. I have had to give up activities like sailing and cycling.

Myoclonus. My legs react to touch and tend to kick out or jerk wildly. This makes dressing and undressing difficult. I cannot 'step out of' a pair of trousers, if dropped to the floor. I cannot bear my feet to be covered in bed. Cold feet are preferable to discomfort.

Falls. Over the last five years, I have fallen, sometimes heavily, and suffered injury. I used to wear hip protectors to cushion effect of falls and to avoid bursitis (swelling) in my hips. On walks, when I dared and was having a good legs day, a lack of manoeuvrability makes me susceptible to vehicles passing too close and a few times I have been knocked over by slipstream. Uneven road surfaces, downhill slopes and sudden gusts of wind can also cause a loss of balance and a fall. Most alarming are backwards falls where there is nothing to slow my descent. Some falls have landed me in hospital, but now I go only if I have lost consciousness, feel diabolical or have bleeding that shows no sign of easing. Otherwise, I get on with it. (Graphic results of some falls, are at the end in Annex 1.)

Involuntary hand movements and coordination. I have sudden, unpredictable, uncontrollable, jerky, and involuntary hand movements. I have difficulty dressing and undressing the lack of fine movement control means I struggle with buttons and zips and I have wet myself on occasions. I usually don't bother to zip up my fly. Also fitting insulin needles, changing hearing aid batteries, using a blood glucose tester and writing, are other areas of challenge. Eating too is difficult with uncooperative hands. I use a small, long handled sundae spoon, as it is the most efficient tool and food is served in a bowl as on a plate it tends to go walkabout. Occasionally I need to be fed.

Gripping objects. I cannot pick up small objects with my left hand. My right has difficulty doing this too. Most attempts to pick up more than one object at once result in one or all to be dropped. Tablets can be difficult to dispense. Unless I am lucky, they find their way to the ground. Practicing all of these is my relearning process, or rehabilitation.

Pain, tingling and sensitivity in feet and hands. This can creep up towards the end of an afternoon and most evenings Sensitivity can prevent sleep. The sensation is like having a flame played on my hands and/or feet. I cannot bear to have anything touching a hand or when at its worst, to rest them on anything.

Feverish sensations in temple. It is quite normal for me to be sweaty and uncomfortable, but without a fever.

Spatial awareness: I frequently knock over items whilst trying to move something. This is more than clumsiness. I misjudge distances or positioning of objects. Before FND I had very good coordination and spatial awareness. I had played the guitar since I was 17, I could juggle and was reasonably competent at DIY. I am now unable to do any of these, though I have restarted playing my guitars, with some success.

Sleep variation. I have no steady pattern of sleep. I can be awake until late into the night, then wake early or sleep into the morning. No consistent sleep pattern emerged for a long time, though my average night has been around six hours for the last several years.

Stamina. Since FND my stamina has been limited. This improved a little after a couple of years with steady and concerted effort. I try to walk daily, with my stroller, when I can. If I overdo it, it means several days' rest, possibly in bed, without the energy to do much. In November 2020, my legs decided not to function, save for indoors or short distances outside. My daily average steps dropped dramatically and only started to show any improvement after a year or so.

Fatigue. This is a constant. Even without any exertion or a walk, I get physically 'spent' by early evening. Occasionally I am unable to lift my legs into bed through tiredness.

Functional or dissociative seizures. Thankfully, these have been, in remission for over a year but were most distressing when they happened.

For me, the trigger was stress, anxiety response, pain, sudden sound, noise, light or touch and occasionally anticipatory reactions to (real or perceived) danger or peril. My body went into a form of stasis, completely unable to move. Senses of touch and hearing were not affected but I couldn't move, nor speak, nor open my eyes. The seizures lasted from around ten minutes, with the longest about five hours. The ambulance service and paramedics attended on many occasions, if just to get me up from the floor.

Weight, BMI and insulin. In the three years after November 2016 when my FND was triggered, my weight dropped steadily without other apparent reason. I shed about 20 Kg and now to maintain my body mass I must supplement meals with protein shakes. My requirement for insulin also dropped from almost 110 insulin units a day to around 30 to 40.

Emotions. I now have a very low emotional threshold.

Emotional spikes, particularly an unsustainable emotional burden and anxiety attacks combined and conspired to trigger functional seizures.

The expansion of this area of my consciousness has enriched my life, quite significantly.

FND Hope International

OK, time for a big fanfare and some serious team talk.

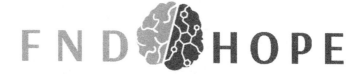

FND Hope proudly is the first and currently the only global patient-led charity for people suffering with FND. It originated as a grassroots campaign, with a mission to uncover the hidden world of FND and to empower those affected with the disorder to live their best possible life.

FND Hope, broadly has dual, parallel missions. Widely to educate about the disorder and to support the community of sufferers wherever they are. We are volunteers. Our growth comes from within, or sometimes with specialist help from responsibly minded and motivated professionals. We draw on whatever strength and learning that we can muster to advance. Together.

There are many reasons for our success, but the following quotation sums up the attitude and motivation for many members of FND

Hope, particularly those who serve on Boards, as Admins in our Facebook support groups, or as Peer Support workers.

"We do these things not because they are easy. We do them because they are hard." John F. Kennedy, on announcing that the USA would, by the end of the 1960s, put a man on the moon and return him safely to earth.

FND Hope International and me

I heard a clarion call to action.

John F Kennedy again, from his inaugural address, January 1961, *"Ask not what America can do for you. Ask what you can do for America."*

I realised that I might be able to do something.

"Though wise men at their end know dark is right,
Because their words had forked no lightning, they
Do not go gentle into that good night."
Dylan Thomas, Do not go gentle into that good night.

Whilst this may seem to be shameless, I knew that I needed to fork some lightning before I go gentle (or kicking and screaming) into the good night.

How did it all come about?

After following and contributing to FND Hope Facebook groups for a couple of months, one day I thought '*I wonder if they could use another volunteer? Even a past sell-by date recycled Buddhist, Welsh hippie lawyer?*' Thus, in a moment of unusual prescience, generosity and, in retrospect, inspiration, I volunteered with an expectation of being asked to do little more than occasionally shake a bucket outside Tesco's.

Fate dictated that this was not to be.

FND Hope contacted me to ask for a full resumé. I decided not to omit anything. Not my bipolar, not my diabetes, not my experiences with cancer. Not the stigma of dismissal from good jobs simply because of a diagnosis. Nothing whatsoever omitted. I even dared to inject some humour, usually fatal in a job CV.

I sent it and waited, anticipating that it would be the last thing I heard! Within just a few days I received an invitation to attend an on-line interview with Bridget Mildon, the founder, inspirational leader, and CEO of FND Hope International.

This raised my eyebrows a little.

A week later and Bridget and I spoke for a couple of hours over a Zoom call. It appeared that my candour about my medical history, particularly as it involved direct personal experience of coping with three chronic disorders (bipolar, diabetes and FND) and that I knew first-hand how much stigma affects sufferers, all was entirely relevant, indeed a positive bonus.

At the end of the interview Bridget asked me if I would be prepared to sit on the FND Hope International Board of Directors, as Legal Advisor.

FND Hope Volunteer Spotlight

ROBERT WILSON THOMAS

Director, Co-chair and Legal Advisor FND Hope International, Trustee and Legal Advisor, FND Hope UK

Lives in the UK
Diagnosed with FND

Robert is Welsh, a Buddhist, bipolar, a barrister since 1977, and now an ardent FND advocate, dedicated to lifting the blanket of general ignorance about FND and the stigma that attends it.

His professional life included large value agreements, team leader in the peace stabilization force in Bosnia, and advising 13 Central and Eastern European Governments on EU joining requirements.

He has have written over twenty books, for none of which he claims any literary merit.

FND HOPE

So much for rattling a bucket outside Tesco's.

I accepted Bridget's offer without hesitating. It was not very much later that I realised that I had come home. I see that much of my professional and personal history is relevant to the role. The coming months brought another invitation, to join the FND Hope UK board as a trustee and also as legal advisor. I have since also taken on the role of data protection officer, for the UK.

I am honoured to be on the Boards of FND Hope International and FND Hope UK and now to be an Admin for more than half a dozen FND Hope Facebook Support Groups. Together, the work this generates is very varied. Everything from disputes, inter affiliate agreements and service supplier contracts to advocacy letters and member support, through policy drafting and amending, data protection and even my beloved intellectual property rights.

I must have done something right as in early 2021 and out of the blue, Bridget called and told me that the International Board wished to invite me to act as Co-Chair of FND Hope International. Another no-brainer, although I did request and take a weekend to mull it over.

Personally, I know that, for me, it is not about <u>being part</u> of FND Hope. It is about *being* FND Hope, in the first person. We are a small, dedicated, and growing group, dedicated to a goal and a mission. Our diagnoses (most of us have FND, some very much affected, some whose symptoms vary wildly) mean that all understand first-hand just what the disorder means.

I am not *a member of* FND Hope. I consider that in my actions, I *am* FND Hope.

My FND Hope colleagues, whether in the USA, UK, Australia or elsewhere seem to share this spirit. This has some limitations, but, as with the disorder itself, finding ways around our lack of ability, finding ways to cope, and still to achieve so much, whilst being a challenge, truly is an honour, not a burden.

I <u>am</u> FND Hope.

Next step?

For me it is establishing a new FND Hope International National Organisation in Ireland. We are in the wilderness here, with little by way of professional support and even the website of the State's health service has but three references to FND, all typos for find! A search for Functional Neurological Disorder brings up a reference to the disorder, under a list of Medically Unexplained Diseases.

This is not good enough.

There has been a chronic lack of neurologists and other professionals in the State for over a decade. There are a few, but too few. The general knowledge of the existence of FND seems almost absent, among first responders, triage staff in A&E, GPs and other doctors. Many neurologists do not recognise the disorder.

I have found that there is far more knowledge and understanding among physiotherapists and some Occupational Therapists, which is the standard among the rest of the medical profession in Ireland.

FND Hope Ireland has a mission to change this.

Our first stage, the FND Hope Ireland Facebook Peer Support Group, launched on 1st April 2022. A most auspicious date as it coincided with the start of the 2022 World FND Awareness Month, 2022.

We are moving!

Peers and friendships

Over the years since I started posting on FND Hope Facebook groups, from time to time, rather frequently in fact, I have had many engaging and quite in-depth private exchanges with other sufferers. These have been with a very wonderfully wide cross section of people and irrespective of gender, age, sexual orientation, race or ethnic origin, degree of disability, nationality, social position, or status. FND Hope, or rather FND itself, really does not discriminate against anyone.

Some of these exchanges lasted a couple of months, some have endured over several years, some last a few days or a handful of exchanged messages, but I regard a good few of these great people as real friends and confidants, although I have yet to meet any of them face to face. I hope that that too will happen in time.

I cherish these folks. I am the better for knowing them. Being able to share intense areas of my life and being part of theirs, even via social media, is a privilege, as much as how Facebook has brought me back in touch with school friends, after a half century gap.

Going back to my previous life

I frequently see posts on the FND Hope Facebook peer-support groups from people who wish that they could go back to how their life was 'before FND'. This is an understandable reaction and as it is shared by so many, here are my thoughts.

By the time I was about 12 or 13 my feet were already UK size 9. I still had little problem finding shops offering a range of footwear that fitted and were attractive. My feet kept growing. By sixteen, they were size 11 and they grew to size 12. Now, most of my shoes are size 13, or, if I am lucky enough to find them, a very wide size 12. Rarely, over for the last 40 years, has a shop offered me a wide selection of footwear.

Yes, naturally I would like to have the size 9 or 10 feet, I had before they grew too big. Similarly, I dearly would like to walk without a stroller, to run, to swim and surf, to ride my bike, to sail my boat. You may bet that I would like all these things. I am not so naïve as to believe that wishing will make it happen.

Then again, doing nothing, just standing still is tantamount to retreating. I now look at new horizons and say, 'How can I go further?' or 'How may I find a more pleasant road?' or even 'Will I meet somebody new today?' This is my 'normal'. I have accepted it and I look for ways to move on, or if needs must, to get around or over.

FND and Relationships

Relationships and FND are a very tricky area. Like the disorder itself, there is no single, simple answer. It is true that relationships rarely are free of problems. Circumstances have made me realise that the lack of essential ability is like the crooked card game. Everyone knows the game is crooked, but it is the only game in town.

Lessons for FND

Solutions

Solutions come from unexpected angles. Relearning something is a technique. You may need help and guidance and the wisdom and experience of others, particularly professional guidance.

You also need to be determined and resilient. Fall seven times, get up eight. There's quite a lot of that.

Things that might help

These are some of my own observations and some that I have gleaned from posts on FND Hope Facebook groups.

Actions like

Taking action based on empathy. This is different to sympathy: that is found in a dictionary between '*shit*' and '*syphilis*'! True empathy hurts.

Proximity, during and immediately after a functional seizure. This is under the head of *comfort and reassurance.* It makes a significant difference.

Susie Lurcher knows and practices this one.

Use soft words and encouragement. This is far and away better than offering subjective, erroneous observations and unsolicited and generally unhelpful advice.

Understand that a late excuse for a no-show is not a slight or discourtesy. Usually there is a good reason, it is regretted but sadly it may be inevitable.

Remember to invite someone, even if unlikely to attend. Inclusion is of itself great reassurance that you exist and are not forgotten.

Taking the time to make an occasional phone call or send a message helps considerably. That is not losing touch, something only too often the case, among so-called friends but also family members. I wonder whether they are ever so busy.

Keeping your word when you promise something. If you are struggling and hanging on, being disappointed can provoke a disproportionately large emotional reaction.

Recognise that a trivial task may have taken a large effort by someone with FND. Yes, it really did take me two hours and a mid-task nap to wash the dishes!

"I believe you" is the most potent and effective response to someone telling a medical professional, or anyone, that they suffer with functional seizures.

Some general self-helpers

Establish a healthy routine. This helps to avoid unpleasant surprises.

Journaling. This has several benefits. It may reveal a trend in symptoms. Medical professionals usually like such records to support you in a consultation.

Use good use of social media and self-help or peer support groups. These may vary in effectiveness, depending on the participants. Some subjects attract negativity, some are a magnet for supporting noises. Occasionally you may get a solution to a problem. Any need to elaborate?

Find medical professionals who understand FND and take time to care. These are as common as hen's teeth, but when you discover one, they are like gold dust.

Rest and relaxation. This is overlooked too often. It is not defeatist, nor lazy. It is essential self-care.

Enjoy and develop conversation. This will provide amity and reassurance. It is also particularly helpful to lift a corner of the blanket of general ignorance that cloaks FND.

Be mindful. The concept of mindfulness has been around forever. Awareness of the benefits of mindful behaviour is relatively recent. It has become a feature of many therapies, from meditation to yoga, to simply being where you are and appreciating everything you can sense around you. Having to develop mindfulness was a gift of my FND. I now can marvel at the range of colours, smells, sounds and feelings, even taste and texture if blackberries are in season, whilst out walking.

The core attributes of mindfulness are non-judging, acceptance, patience, maintaining a beginner's mind, having trust, being non-striving, letting go and feeling and living gratitude. Jon Kabat-Zinn's book on mindfulness, Full Catastrophe Living, available on Amazon, though a bit long and detailed can be recommended.

Take whatever exercise you can. This should go without saying. The benefits for physical health and mental well-being have been known for years. If you can no longer run, walk or dance, there are chair exercises. My neuro-physio has introduced me to several exercises to improve my balance and gait. Some are straightforward. Others are the very devil. Sensing a bit of a glow helps me feel justified and positive.

Carers and unsolicited offers to help

Personally, I try to do as much as can, as often as possible, and as 'normally' as I am able. The next time I may need to.

OK, so I fail. I admit that I fall, I spill and break things, but however this makes me feel, I am determined never to give up, Then, an uninvited intervention, no matter how kind and well intentioned, makes me more determined to succeed, and to do so by myself. I have upset people by pushing away such unwanted intrusions.

I spend a lot of time thinking about and planning how to achieve something without anyone to help. How, for instance would I go from here, in Ireland to the middle of Europe? What workaround would I need to stay in a hotel without disabled facilities. How would I shop, cook, eat and do what else I would need?

This is my very self-centred way to go. Sailing singled-handed or with a minimum or mainly seasick and disinterested crew, taught me a lot about this.

Now before anyone tears off my face, let me make it clear that accepting help IS OK, so long as it is not prefaced by '*let me do that for you*', and particularly if it is delivered in a '*I can't wait for you all day*' tone. Much better is to be asked '*do you need/want help?*' or better '*how may I help you?*' The latter is great if the helper listens and does what you say what help you need or want.

Alternatively, if you ask for help, explaining what you NEED then the 'helper' does something else, I find extremely provocative.

My advice is, with anything but a casual offer of help, is to explain your limitations and to ask for support and assistance to help YOU to achieve an end. Make them aware, softly but firmly, that when you are struggling with something, you may be about to succeed. Taking over would rob you of the success and satisfaction. It will also prevent your remembering the next time that you did it before, so you know you can do it again!

You may find that these suggestions are not always well received. You need to be clear that you do your best, but this will not be possible if others, however motivated, try and but in and do things for you. They may not be there the next time.

Becoming overwhelmed

When we are at our lowest life states, everything seems impossible, even getting out of bed some mornings. You may find your energy and motivation barely enough to get by.

If you asked yourself "What are you struggling with?" you might conclude that it is everything, or even life itself. This is just a blanket observation and if you were to look more deeply at what exactly is worrying about *right now,* or what you are finding overwhelming, right now, you might just realise that the real issue could be staring right at you.

Take the example of washing up.

When you have managed to prepare a meal and have eaten it, you may have run out of energy, so you leave the dishes in the sink. No big deal until there is a sink full of dirty plates and mugs but none on the shelf. You have a dishwasher but lack the energy to load it. Assuming you can get your bum in gear, you throw all the plates and things into the machine and run it. Because food remains are dried on, they emerge still dirty.

Here's the problem: You don't want to scrub the dishes by hand and the dishwasher can't cope. Is there a solution?

How about running the dishwasher twice?

I know that the manufacturers tell you that you shouldn't do this, but we know that a first wash may clear surface dirt, a second gets down to the stuck-on stuff and if needs be, a third wash gets them spotless.

Why does this work for your problem? Simply recognise that *there are no rules.*

Run the dishwasher twice, rinse and repeat. If it works for you, ignore the messages, internal and external that say '*you shouldn't do this*' or '*you should always do that*'!

Gratitude – a great teacher

This should be the ground floor of every action you take, each thought you make and every word you utter. It is ridiculously hard, may seem impossible. It takes practice, plenty of practice.

The returns and rewards are many times the effort that you invest.

Pace yourself

This is something that I am particularly bad at. I often go at
something and completely run out of juice before I realise it. Pacing
is more than important, it is vital. Find your limits, perhaps push
them a little, but do not ignore them completely.

There is a word that frequently is used in this context: spoons or
spoonies,

Being a Spoonie (*and in the wider FND community we take some
pride in this gentle moniker*) means counting imaginary teaspoons.
Imagine that you have a tray of teaspoons. Each teaspoon represents
a unit of energy available to your body. Each daily task takes an
amount of energy, or a number of spoons. It is for you to allot your
daily 'spoons' to your activities, remembering that the number of
spoons available is finite and that they can and do run out.

This is one relatively simple way to pace yourself. There is much
more about this on the FND Hope website. (*Go look!*)

Grounding

This is a technique we can adopt to mitigate or head off an
escalation of FND symptoms. It includes mindfulness, distraction,
finger tapping and some gentle physical activity. It is another
essential skill about which there is much more on the FND Hope
website. (*Again, go look!*)

Recently I discovered that I can sometimes coax my legs into
movement through singing a song to myself. My song? The Great
Escape March. Aside from being an enjoyable piece of music, the
concept of escape is not entirely lost on me.

OK, it's a bit corny, but if it works…

Things that don't help

Uninformed commentary

This is an uninformed comment such as any of these beauties:

"Have you tried …?" (*Just insert your pet hate –the latest celebrity diet is one of my major peeves!*)

"I had a headache/migraine/faint/fall once." (*Oh really? Did it last for weeks/months/years? Did you tumble multiple times a day?*)

"Just snap out of it." (*Eugh! Give me strength! The only thing to be snapped out of is a garden pea from a pod!*)

"You look great, how can you say you are ill?" (*Because dummkopf, perhaps I might just be ill, or because I really AM ill! It is an invisible disability.*)

"It must be great hanging around at home all day!" (*You mean when I am not furniture surfing to get to the loo in time?*)

"It's all in your head." (*So are my eyes and ears, but in any case, how in the name of Noah's testicles would you know?*)

"FND isn't like a real illness." (*Utter bollocks!*)

Inappropriate or thoughtless actions

Being ignored or shunned.

Having physical pain inflicted. (This is particularly so if the pain is inflicted by a first responder to prove a misguided and groundless pet theory that you are shamming or that a functional seizure is being put on).

Blaming, shaming or making hollow accusations and vulgar insults. (Whilst sticks and stones may break my bones, we are vulnerable to these names which can hurt us!).

Gossiping. (It is not in the least true what Oscar Wilde said, *"that the only thing worse than being talked about is NOT being talked about"*)

Deliberately or unthinkingly making noise. (*Give me peace!*)

Disrupting carefully planned activity. (It is neither clever nor funny when a carefully thought-out a way around an obstacle is stymied by an intervention that moves it.)

Offering help and refusing to accept how best to do so. ("*How can I help*" if you insist, please!)

Refusing to recognise or ignoring obvious and unmistakeable signals (*such as exhaustion, lack of appetite, isolation*).

Stressors such as

Anxiety. (This is a constant battle that we conduct with ourselves!)

Pointless and petty arguments or point scoring. (A battle that we conduct with others!)

Third party pressure and arbitrary deadlines. (Remember there are no rules! Run the dishwasher twice!)

Unrealistic goals. (Our own or those of other people!)

Abandonment, or threatened abandonment. (We need security, or sometimes just the appearance of it!)

Interruption of routine. (This may throw us right out of equilibrium!)

Threats of and actual violence. (Does this really need elaboration?)

Buddhism

I have left this to the end quite deliberately as, whilst it has evolved over time, it marks the map, compass, and the walking stick that most has supported me during my life and particularly over the last thirty-seven years on my varied and eventful journey.

How my spiritual journey began.

I was brought up in the Church in Wales and a regular churchgoer until I went to university. When still young I was challenged by an aged relative to say if I believed in God. I had never given this a thought, save that from the way the question was asked I knew the answer that was expected.

I persisted in telling myself the same answer, blindly, but, even whilst I went to church, I had doubts. Convention overrode these doubts for over a decade. I had no way to know, nor had anyone to discuss or challenge them. For some years I was an altar server and had the dubious distinction of passing out one Christmas morning resulting in a trip to A&E to have the cut on my head stitched.

For some years, I contemplated becoming a clergyman, more from a lack of a clear idea about what I wanted from life than as a calling. It was a convenient shelter from the career master's questions. I was dissuaded (by the then Bishop of Swansea and Brecon) from taking this path until after university. The idea evaporated after I left home.

My cloistered 'Christian', beliefs drifted away from both the church and over time, from a generally theist philosophy. I was appalled by the elitist behaviour of the Christian Students' Association. They ignored or shunned anyone not a member of their coven, to the point of direct rudeness. This was not Christianity. It was the bigotry of '*love thy neighbour but only if he is in the same elitist clique*'.

Too many wars have been fought over belief. Too few disputes have been resolved from accepting and cherishing the differences that appear to divide us.

After my faith evaporated, I enjoyed a period of agnosticism that led to settled atheism although it was a few years until the latter crystalised.

I wondered about other religions, with no-one to ask for information. There was too little sufficient to take me further. After reading several Herman Hesse books, dedicated to 'The Journeyers in the East', I thought about Zen Buddhism, but it was a passing thought.

General philosophy

I have been a pacifist since I was a teen. My pacifism is founded on '*pace*' (peace) not '*passive*' (inaction). My Christianity vanished about the time I misplaced my virginity. There was no bolt of lightning, nor have I looked back, nor regretted either.

There were few occasions when I went to church, but twice of my own volition, looking for an answer but finding none. Other, that is, than for weddings, Christenings and funerals, or as a tourist.

Sincere (Buddhist) prayers for the future happiness of my Great Uncle Harry, 1082599, L.Bdr, Royal Artillery, Heavy Brigade, killed 14 August, 1944. He was but 35 when he died of his wounds, "*Somewhere in a foreign field...*" Commonwealth War Graves, Florence, September 2002.

I had a self-centred hedonist and spiritually abandoned life through my twenties. I went where I wanted, when I wished to and with whom I chose and did as I wished. Then I began the trail as an alcoholic in making.

I thought, wrongly that this was freedom. It was pleasant but it sowed seeds for later problems.

Buddhism

If you are not interested in how I became a Buddhist or what it is all about, you can skip this chapter, though I hope that you will not.

In June 1984 when I was 32, I met Buddhism, or rather, Buddhism found me. It was at a party to which I was not invited but was taken by what euphemistically is called a *'friend with benefits'*. She met someone else to share her benefits and abandoned me, drunk as a skunk.

I came to the attention of Carol who, I discovered, the hostess had asked to *'watch the drunk gate crasher in case he causes trouble'*.

I recall trying to make polite conversation with Carol, but I was far too pissed to take in much other than that she was a practising Buddhist. She talked about Buddhism. In my 'confused' state I gave her three versions of my phone number hoping she might call me. Fortunately, she opted for the right one and got in touch.

Our relationship lasted ten months. Typical of my relationships, from my selfish view it was mainly physical and with no consideration other than of my desires. I gave little or no thought to her preference, nor considered the future. I even had an interview for a job in Somerset, without mentioning it to Carol.

During my time with Carol, she dragged me 'kicking and screaming' to several Buddhist meetings. On one meeting attended by several hundred young people, I 'sat on my hands' (as she described it) as others in the hall raved through the event.

Ultimately the relationship stopped when Carol saw good sense and left. She had decided, not without reason, that I was a lost cause. I took solace in the bottle. One day about a month later, whilst nursing a colossal hangover, I called her at work and begged to see her, to patch up things. She refused, adding "*You have to do it for yourself. You have the contact numbers for the (Buddhist) group.*"

Why I called the number, to this day I do not know. I am extremely glad that I did. I met two leaders and we chatted about my 'problems'. They responded to all, drawing on Buddhist philosophy, which made perfect theoretical sense, though they stressed that any answer was down to me, to only to me.

Against type, I took a leap of trust to see if Buddhism was for me.

I admit that all I wanted was some company, specifically female company and not for polite conversation, a meal out or a theatre trip. I also thought about proof that 'it' worked and that I might develop faith. I was comfortable with what I had read on the theory and the literature made sense. In starting to chant I entered a new realm.

I chanted to find faith, nothing else. I thought I would give it six months. Perhaps all I wanted was something, anything, in which to believe.

It is the answer, I found, but this realisation developed over years. It is ironic that chanting is, of itself an act of pure faith, so my first prayers were answered immediately.

Basic principles

I would like to share a basic principle. It may strike a chord in your life, as they did in mine.

The purpose of Buddhism is simple. *"To become happy!"*

This is the start and the end of the practice. That's the basic tenet. I have included more details in Annex 2.

Influences

Parents and parenting

Music

Teach your Children, Crosby, Stills, Nash and Young, Deja Vu.
The best track on the finest LP of all time. The concept of parents
learning from their children was wholly lost on my parents.

Poetry

This be the Verse, by Philip Larkin (1922 –1985)
They fuck you up, your mum and dad.
They may not mean to, but they do.
They fill you with the faults they had
And add some extra, just for you.

But they were fucked up in their turn
By fools in old-style hats and coats,
Who half the time were soppy-stern
And half at one another's throats.

Man hands on misery to man.
It deepens like a coastal shelf.
Get out as early as you can,
And don't have any kids yourself.

No Man is an Island John Donne, (1572-1631)
"No man is an island entire of itself;
every man is a piece of the continent, a part of the main;
if a clod be washed away by the sea, Europe is the less, as well as if
a promontory were, as well as any manner of thy friends or of thine
own were;
any man's death diminishes me, because I am involved in mankind.
And therefore never send to know for whom the bell tolls; it tolls for
thee."

Meditation XVII, Devotions upon Emergent Occasions

Quotations

"Children begin by loving their parents; after a time, they judge them; rarely, if ever, do they forgive them."
Oscar Wilde.

"The real meaning of youth has nothing to do with physical age. In Buddhist terms, youth means consistently to maintain an open, flexible and tolerant mind."
Daisaku Ikeda.

Education, School and afterwards

Quotations

"Education at its best is a process of liberation from prejudice which frees the human heart from its violent passions. Through education people can be delivered from powerlessness, from the burden of mistrust directed against themselves."
Daisaku Ikeda.

"A teacher I once had told me that the older you get, the lonelier you become and the deeper the love you need."
Leonard Cohen.

Films

Seize the Day, and **Patch Adams**, both Robin Williams.

Books

The Glass Bead Game, Hermann Hesse.

A book for anyone interested in the universality of intellect. This is my 50-year-old, battered, treasured and much-read volume.

Legal career

Poetry

Six Honest Serving-Men, Rudyard Kipling (in "**Just So Stories**")

I keep six honest serving-men
(They taught me all I knew);
Their names are What and Why and When
And How and Where and Who.

Quotations

"Never ask a question on cross examination to which you do not know the answer."
Origin somewhat unclear but it was used in a similar form by Harper Lee in *To Kill a Mockingbird*. In any case it is frequently cited as the first rule of advocacy.

"Never fuck a colleague."
Max Aitkin, 1st Baron Beaverbrook, to a young journalist who asked him for some career advice. This short, crude and blunt answer is quite deep as there are two ways of interpreting it. Physically or professionally.

I did the first, once or perhaps twice, and regretted it. The second has been done to me, on a few occasions. It is by far the worse of the two, and by a very long chalk.

Films

Twelve Angry Men, Henry Fonda, and a clutch of other fine actors in the quintessential Jury Room film.

Witness for the Prosecution, Charles Laughton, Tyrone Power, Marlene Dietrich, and Elsa Lanchester. Directed by Billy Wilder this is one of the best and most enjoyable English courtroom dramas.

Books

The Politics of the Judiciary, John Aneurin Grey Griffith's classic account of how, whilst the judiciary cannot act other than neutrally, in practice it must (and does) act politically.

People

Michael Fysh. My second pupil master, an outstanding advocate in intellectual property rights, my co-author and humble enough to listen to and learn from his lowly pupil.

Health and Wellness

Quotations

"For those who understand, no explanation is needed.
For those who do not understand, no explanation is possible."
Anon.

"[...] the only people for me are the mad ones, the ones who are mad to live, mad to talk, mad to be saved, desirous of everything at the same time, the ones who never yawn or say a commonplace thing, but burn, burn, burn like fabulous yellow roman candles exploding like spiders across the stars and in the middle you see the blue centerlight pop and everybody goes 'Awww!'."
Jack Kerouac, On the Road

"I think that the saddest people always try their hardest to make people happy. Because they know what it's like to feel absolutely worthless and they don't want anybody else to feel like that,"
Robin Williams (1951 to 2014)

"Illness can motivate us to take stock of ourselves, to reflect on the essence of life and our way of living. Through struggling with illness, we gain a much fuller understanding of life and forge spiritual strength,"
Daisaku Ikeda.

Films

Reach for the Sky. Kenneth More.
The inspirational and true story of Douglas Bader, WW2 fighter
pilot, who lost both legs in a flying accident ten years before.
Coincidentally, his artificial legs were fitted in Roehampton
Hospital which today is home to the neurorehabilitation centre of the
Wolfson Unit (part of the St George's Hospital, Tooting).

One Flew Over the Cuckoo's nest, Jack Nicholson.
Profoundly sad depiction of how mentally ill patients were treated
(or more correctly, mis-treated) in a mental asylum. From personal
experience, but to a much lesser extent, the abuse continues in one
way or another in many institutions today.

Books

You are not Alone, Title of a booklet as an introduction to mental
health by the UK charity Mind. The very first spring of comfort and
hope, post bipolar diagnosis. I no longer felt like Frankenstein's
monster – the only one of a kind.

I often use the phrase on FND Hope's Peer Support Facebook
Groups.

People in my life

Professor Mark Edwards, consultant neurologist. Diagnosed my
FND and enabled/enables me to think outside the FND box.

Glenn Neilson, neuro-physiotherapist. Conducted my neuro-physio
in 2017. Gave me true hope that I could walk again, though this was
and always will be down to my own personal motivation and
persistence. *"If you want to walk, you must practice walking."*

Professor Michael Walsh, a most competent and rather unassuming, but great Irish surgeon who helped me say goodbye to my throat cancer.

Bridget Mildon, Founder and CEO of FND Hope International. An inspiration. A colleague. A friend who saw and recognised that my experience living with bipolar disorder and stigma were relevant to understanding and helping people with FND.

This helped to restore my faith in myself, more than I could have imagined.

Activities

Poetry

Do not go gentle into that good night, Dylan Thomas (1914 – 1953)

"*Do not go gentle into that good night,*
Old age should burn and rave at close of day;
Rage, rage against the dying of the light.

Though wise men at their end know dark is right,
Because their words had forked no lightning they
Do not go gentle into that good night.

Good men, the last wave by, crying how bright
Their frail deeds might have danced in a green bay,
Rage, rage against the dying of the light.

Wild men who caught and sang the sun in flight,
And learn, too late, they grieved it on its way,
Do not go gentle into that good night.

Grave men, near death, who see with blinding sight
Blind eyes could blaze like meteors and be gay,
Rage, rage against the dying of the light.

And you, my father, there on the sad height,
Curse, bless, me now with your fierce tears, I pray.
Do not go gentle into that good night.
Rage, rage against the dying of the light. "

Written in 1951 to his father, D.W. Thomas, as he approached
blindness and death. The poem reveals an aspect of the relationship
between Dylan and his father and a profound respect for his father's
uncompromising independence of mind and how it was tamed by
illness.

Quotations

"Man cannot discover new oceans unless he has the courage to lose
sight of the shore."
André Gide

"Courage is not having the strength to go on; it is going on when
you don't have the strength."
Theodore Roosevelt.

"In harbour a ship is safe. That is not why men build ships. "
I remember this on a poster in my little sister's bedroom.

To this I would add my complete and unshakable admiration for the
heroic men and women who man RNLI vessels around the British
Isles, and who go out when seasoned seaman come in.

Books

Seven Pillars of Wisdom, T.E. Lawrence.
The autobiographical account of the experiences of Lawrence of Arabia while serving as a liaison officer with rebel forces during the Arab Revolt of 1916 to 1918 against the Ottoman Turks.

Sex, Drugs and Rock and Roll

Music

Woodstock, 1969. Start to finish. In particular:
White Rabbit, Jefferson Airplane
"Remember what the white mouse said: Feed your head"

All Along the Watchtower, Jimi Hendrix.
Among my favourite of Bob Dylan's songs, and my favourite interpretation of it.

Will You? Hazel O'Connor.
Could this have the greatest saxophone solo of all time? The lyrics are poignant too and reminiscent of not a few similar encounters. 4 minutes and 49 seconds of angels copulating in my mind.

Quotations

"If you remember the 60s, you weren't there"
Comedian Charlie Fleischer, Los Angeles Times, 1982.

I can remember some bits. Some are a bit foggy. I go back in my dreams, from time to time.

Films

Easy Rider, 1969, Peter Fonda, Dennis Hopper and Jack Nicholson.
A landmark film, and a touchstone for the generation that turned on,

tuned in and dropped out. It captured the imagination and zeitgeist of the era. The film explores the societal landscape, issues, and tensions in the USA in the 1960s, focussing on the rise of the hippie movement, drug use, and a communal lifestyle. The music is great too, even over half a century later.

Woodstock, 1970. American documentary film of the watershed counterculture Festival of the title, in August 1969 near Bethel, New York. THE event that just about everyone, of my generation wished that they had been at. Rolling Stone magazine called it *'the benchmark of concert movies and one of the most entertaining documentaries ever made'.*

Books

Brave New World, Aldous Huxley. *"A gram is better than a damn".*

Marriage, love and thereafter

Music

The Rose, Bette Midler. *'... love is only for the lucky and the strong'.*

Wasn't Born to Follow, Byrds. An Easy Rider track, although the acoustic version by Tal Hurley is at least as good, if not, possibly a little better, not the least for having all the verses.

Tomorrow is such a long time, Bob Dylan.
Arguably one of Dylan's greatest love songs, if a little-known number.

Poetry

The Winners, Rudyard Kipling
If you think you are beaten, you are.
If you think you dare not, you don't
If you like to win but think you can't,
It's almost a cinch you won't.

If you think you'll lose, you're lost.
For out in the world we find
Success begins with a fellow's will
It's all in the state of mind.

If you think you are outclassed, you are.
You've got to think high to rise.
You've got to be sure of yourself before
You can ever win the prize.

Life's battles don't always go
To the stronger or faster man.
But sooner or later, the man who wins
Is the man who thinks he can.

"What the moral? Who rides may read.
When the night is thick and the tracks are blind
A friend at a pinch is a friend, indeed,
But a fool to wait for the laggard behind.
Down to Gehenna or up to the Throne,
He travels the fastest who travels alone.

White hands cling to the tightened rein,
Slipping the spur from the booted heel,
Tenderest voices cry " Turn again!"
Red lips tarnish the scabbarded steel,
High hopes faint on a warm hearth-stone--
He travels the fastest who travels alone.

One may fall but he falls by himself--

Falls by himself with himself to blame.
One may attain and to him is pelf--
Loot of the city in Gold or Fame.
Plunder of earth shall be all his own
Who travels the fastest and travels alone.

Wherefore the more ye be holpen and stayed,
Stayed by a friend in the hour of toil,
Sing the heretical song I have made--
His be the labour and yours be the spoil.
Win by his aid and the aid disown--
He travels the fastest who travels alone!"

Quotations

"It may be true that he travels farthest who travels alone, but the goal thus reached is not worth reaching."
Theodore Roosevelt, as a counter to Kipling's observation.

People

Too many to mention, though I love or loved you all, one way or another, in my own way. If I never told you, I should have.

Travelling and flying

Quotations

"Be ready when your opportunity arrives"
Benjamin Disraeli.

"Go whilst the going is good."
Uncredited, of British origin. Used, in part, by Evelyn Waugh as the title of his book about his travels and adventures in Abyssinia.

"He who travels furthest travels alone"
Rudyard Kipling.

"My toes too numb to step, wait only for my boot heels to be following...".
Bob Dylan, Mr Tambourine Man

Books

As Far as My Feet will Carry Me, Josef Martin Bauer.
The escape from a Siberian Gulag and journey back to Germany by a World War II prisoner of war.

People

Carl Knutson, for awakening me to the fact that the main reason to travel is to meet people of different cultures.

Emotions

Poetry

Two poems by Dylan Thomas.

Do not go gentle into that good night. Still packs the enormous impact that it did when first I read it.
"Rage, rage against the dying of the light."

And death shall have no dominion. Poignant, rebellious and philosophical. Moving and inspirational.

Films

The Cruel Sea, specifically the scene where Jack Hawkins, openly weeps, something that, at the time, was not expected of strong male leading actors.

Real men do cry. We each have our limits.

People

Too many again but, in general all those who made me cry, laugh, think, reconsider, love or heal.

Life, Philosophy and Buddhism

Music

Keep right on to the end of the road, Harry Lauder.
Legend has it that Mr Lauder was performing at a music hall during World War 1 when, in the interval he received a telegram telling him that his son had been killed in France. He sang this song to open the second half of the performance. I cannot begin to comprehend how he managed to sing, though perhaps he understood that so many, too many needed to hear the message.

Poetry

War poets

For Johnny, John Pudney

Do not despair
For Johnny-head-in-air;
He sleeps as sound
As Johnny underground.

Fetch out no shroud
For Johnny-in-the-cloud;
And keep your tears
For him in after years.

Better by far

For Johnny-the-bright-star,
To keep your head,
And see his children fed.

In 1940, Pudney was an intelligence officer in the RAF and a member of the Air Ministry's Creative Writer's Unit. He published articles for this unit and wrote considerable poetry, including this famous ode to British airmen. The poem achieved national significance and was broadcast and performed by several famous actors including Sir Laurence Olivier. It was used in the 1945 film "The Way to The Stars"

It is a poem that stirs many senses, and its subject matter is profound and sad yet tinged with hope.

For the Fallen, Lawrence Binyon (1869 – 1943)

"With proud thanksgiving, a mother for her children,
England mourns for her dead across the sea.
Flesh of her flesh they were, spirit of her spirit,
Fallen in the cause of the free.

Solemn the drums thrill; Death august and royal
Sings sorrow up into immortal spheres,
There is music in the midst of desolation
And a glory that shines upon our tears.

They went with songs to the battle, they were young,
Straight of limb, true of eye, steady and aglow.
They were staunch to the end against odds uncounted;
They fell with their faces to the foe.

Age shall not weary them, nor the years condemn.
At the going down of the sun and in the morning
We will remember them.

They mingle not with their laughing comrades again;
They sit no more at familiar tables of home;
They have no lot in our labour of the day-time;

They sleep beyond England's foam.

But where our desires are and our hopes profound,
Felt as a well-spring that is hidden from sight,
To the innermost heart of their own land they are known
As the stars are known to the Night;

As the stars that shall be bright when we are dust,
Moving in marches upon the heavenly plain;
As the stars that are starry in the time of our darkness,
To the end, to the end, they remain."

Too often the fourth stanza is quoted in isolation, although the entire poem is worthy of consideration.

Missing, John Pudney

Less said the better.
The bill unpaid, the dead letter.
No roses at the end
Of Smith, my friend.

Last words don't matter,
And there are none to flatter.
Words will not fill the post
Of Smith, the ghost.

For Smith, our brother,
only son of a loving mother,
The ocean lifted, stirred,
Leaving no word.

The men and women who always will be "Still on watch".

Quotations

"Life is either a daring adventure, or nothing."
Helen Keller

"We hold these truths to be self-evident. That all men are created equal, that they are endowed by their creator with certain inalienable rights; right, liberty and the pursuit of happiness."
American Declaration of Independence.

I learned this in school. It is, to my mind, one of the finest statements of social and political aspiration ever written in English. That the signatories committed sedition by signing the document, which under English law was punishable by death, makes the declaration and the bold statement it embraces, even more remarkable.

"It is not the critic who counts; not the man who points out how the strong man stumbles, or where the doer of deeds could have done them better. The credit belongs to the man who is actually in the arena, whose face is marred by dust and sweat and blood; who strives valiantly; who errs, who comes short again and again, because there is no effort without error and shortcoming; but who does actually strive to do the deeds; who knows great enthusiasms, the great devotions; who spends himself in a worthy cause; who at the best knows in the end the triumph of high achievement, and who at the worst, if he fails, at least fails while daring greatly, so that his place shall never be with those cold and timid souls who neither know victory nor defeat."
Teddy Roosevelt, Speech to the Sorbonne, Paris, 23rd April 1910

"A new era is upon us. Even the lesson of victory itself brings with it profound concern, both for our future security and the survival of civilisation. The destructiveness of the war potential, through progressive advances in scientific discovery, has in fact now reached a point which revises the traditional concept of war.

Men since the beginning of time have sought peace. Various methods through the ages have been attempted to devise an international process to prevent or settle disputes between nations. From the very start workable methods were found in so far as individual citizens were concerned, but the mechanics of an

instrumentality of larger international scope have never been
successful. ~

Military alliances, balances of power, leagues of nations, all in turn
failed, leaving the only path to be by way of the crucible of war. The
utter destructiveness of war now blocks out this alternative. We have
had our last chance. If we will not devise some greater and more
equitable system, our Armageddon will be at our door. The problem
basically is theological and involves a spiritual recrudescence, an
improvement of human character that will synchronize with our
almost matchless advances in science, art, literature, and all
material and cultural developments of the past two thousand years.
It must be of the spirit if we are to save the flesh."
General Douglas Macarthur, 2nd September 1945.

"I have a dream that one day this nation will rise up and live out the
true meaning of its creed: "We hold these truths to be self-evident:
that all men are created equal." I have a dream that one day on the
red hills of Georgia the sons of former slaves and the sons of former
slaveowners will be able to sit down together at a table of
brotherhood. I have a dream that one day even the state of
Mississippi, a desert state, sweltering with the heat of injustice and
oppression, will be transformed into an oasis of freedom and justice.
I have a dream that my four children will one day live in a nation
where they will not be judged by the color of their skin but by the
content of their character. I have a dream today."
Martin Luther King, Jr., 28 August 1963.

"Only one person went to Parliament with good intentions. Guy
Fawkes."
(Anonymous, but often quoted.)

"When the Nazis came for the communists,
I remained silent;
I was not a communist.

When they locked up the social democrats,
I remained silent;
I was not a social democrat.

When they came for the trade unionists,
I did not speak out;
I was not a trade unionist.

When they came for me,
there was no one left to speak out."

Reverend Martin Niemoeller (1892-1984) a German Lutheran
pastor, who in 1938 was arrested by the Gestapo and sent to Dachau.
He survived and was freed by allied forces in 1945.

"Start by doing what's necessary; then do what's possible; and
suddenly you are doing the impossible."
Francis of Assisi.

"No matter what people tell you, words and ideas can change the
world."
Robin Williams (1951 to 2014)

"War does not show who is right. It shows who is left."
Anon.

Films, TV, and Plays

The Dam Busters.
After the successful; raid on the Ruhr dams, at the end of the film,
the leader, Wing Commander Guy Gibson is asked by Barnes
Wallace, inventor of the bouncing bomb and appalled by the loss of
lives among the crews on the raid, *'are you coming to have some*
breakfast?'

Gibson's response reflects the human cost of the raid, *"No, I have*
some letters to write..."

The Accrington Pals, 1981, Peter Whelan.
One of the best plays about WW1. The contradictions of the time, the emotions and the and the late scenes are utterly terrifying. Though it is well over thirty years since I saw it, in Northampton with an amateur dramatic company.

The intense emotional impact has stayed with me.

Blackadder Goes Forth. BBC. Written by Richard Curtis and Ben Elton.

The final scene of the last Blackadder series (Titled '*Goodbyeee*', and first screened 2nd November 1989)

Very similar to the end of The Accrington Pals. The episode notes stated simply '*They go over the top. They don't get very far…*'. For millions of others in the Great War, on both sides, this was the case. Watching it, my heart seems to stop. My tears start. It is the same every time. Truly profound and deeply moving.

Books

1984, George Orwell. "Big Brother is Watching You."

Animal Farm, also George Orwell. "All animals are created equal, except that some are created more equal than others."

Buddhism

Quotations

Nichiren Daishonin

"*…the journey from Kamakura to Kyoto takes twelve days. If you travel for eleven but stop with only one day remaining, how can you*

admire the moon over the capital?"
Letter to Niike

"The hardships along the way were worse than I could have imagined, and indeed more than I can put down in writing. I will leave you to surmise what I endured. But I have been prepared for such difficulties from the outset, so there is no point in starting to complain about them now. I shall accordingly say no more of the matter."
Letter from Teradomari.

"Suffer what there is to suffer, enjoy what there is to enjoy. Regard both suffering and joy as facts of life, and continue chanting Nam-Myoho-Renge-Kyo, no matter what happens. How could this be anything other than the boundless joy of the Law? Strengthen your power of faith more than ever...."
Happiness in this World.

"Believe in this mandala with all your heart. Nam-Myoho-Renge-Kyo is like the roar of a lion. What sickness can therefore be an obstacle?"
Letter to Kyo'o.

Daisaku Ikeda, President, Soka Gakkai International.

"If a person is hungry, we should give them bread. When there is no bread, we can at least give words that nourish. To a person who looks ill or is physically frail, we can turn the conversation to some subject that will lift their spirits and fill them with the hope and determination to get better.

Let us give something to each person we meet: joy, courage, hope, assurance, philosophy, wisdom, a vision for the future. Let us always give something."

"Just as cherry, plum, peach and damson blossoms all possess their own unique qualities, each person is unique. We cannot become

someone else. The important thing is that we live true to ourselves and cause the great flower of our lives to blossom."

"Illness can motivate us to take stock of ourselves, to reflect on the essence of life and our way of living, Through struggling with illness, we can gain a much fuller understanding of life and forge invincible spiritual strength,"

People

Daisaku Ikeda. My mentor in this life and from whom I have learned a great deal.

Carol Rees-Williams. Who courageously and compassionately introduced me to Nam-Myoho-Renge-Kyo and to the correct Buddhist practice.

Dick Causton. Who gently but firmly corrected my frequent mistaken ideas in the early days.

Life, living and non-life.

Quotations

"Ask not what America can do for you. Ask what you can do for America."
John Fitzgerald Kennedy, inaugural address, January 1961.

"Help others and give something back. I guarantee you will discover that while public service improves the lives and the world around you, its greatest reward is the enrichment and new meaning it will bring your own life."
Arnold Schwarzenegger

References

FND and FND Hope

FND Hope home page: www.fndhope.org

The FND Hope open Facebook group:
https://www.facebook.com/FNDHOPE/

The FND Hope YouTube Channel:
https://www.youtube.com/channel/UCrjAQ7hLiP4jgCmFHFuFXF
w

FND Hope on Twitter: @FNDHope @FNDHopeUK

My Twitter handle @Robertwt01

Neurological symptoms, relating to Functional Neurological
Disorder. This, with the FND Hope website, in the 'go to' reference
place. www.neurosymptoms.org

Soka Gakkai International

The source of information about all aspects of Nichiren Buddhism
from the Global lay organisation for practitioners.
https://www.sokaglobal.org/

Mindfulness

Jon Kabat-Zinn's classic book on mindfulness, Full Catastrophe
Living, available on Amazon. Information on the core attitudes of
mindfulness may be found on the Minds Unlimited YouTube
channel at
https://www.youtube.com/channel/UC6E30fgH6ON5lclNHiGlGAQ

Parting words

I hope that you have enjoyed this book and that you have derived some inspiration from reading it.

If I may leave you with a few last words, in Welsh, taken from the refrain the modern folk song written and made famous by a great singer and ardent Welsh nationalist called Dafydd Iwan.

"Er gwaetha pawb a phopeth, Ry'n ni yma o hyd."

"In spite of everyone and everything, we are still here."

We are still here.

Or more personally: *Dw i yma o hyd* – **I am still here.**

Robert WILSON THOMAS
BSc (Hons), Barrister-at-Law.
Co-chair, Director and Legal Advisor,
FND Hope International

Trustee, Legal Advisor and Data Protection Officer,
FND Hope UK

Committee member and Legal Advisor,
FND Hope Ireland

Annex 1 – Injuries

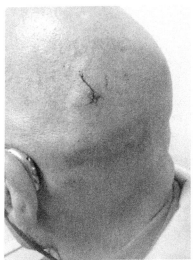

Typical head wounds, of which there have been scores over the first
five years.

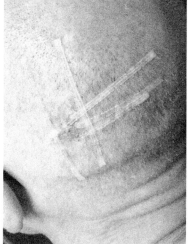

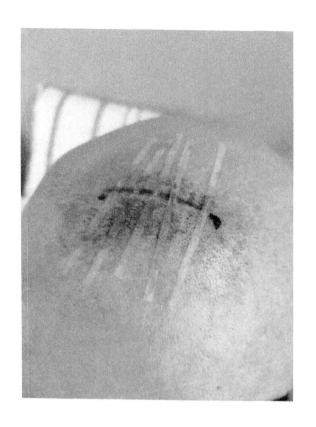

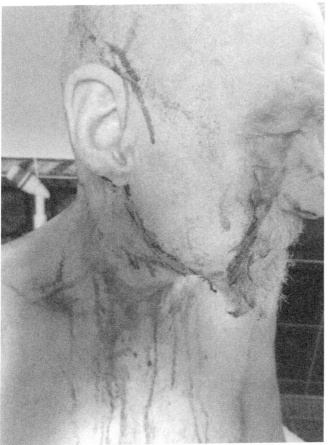

Yes, these are serious falls. The effects of some have been rather dramatic.

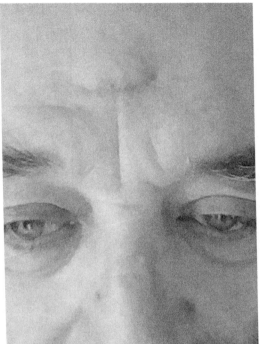

Back, sides and front. I can fall in any direction!

This is the inevitable result of a rather graceless freefall from the half landing to the ground floor. I said several very rude words.

There are also other wounds, mostly resulting in bursitis (swelling) of the elbow (or knee or hip, depending on the point of impact!)

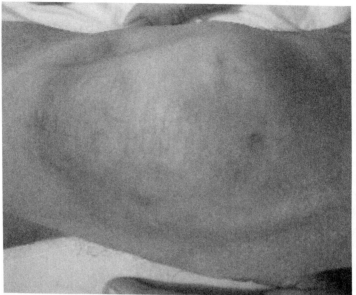

Knee.

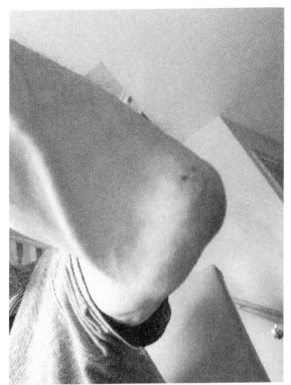

Elbow.

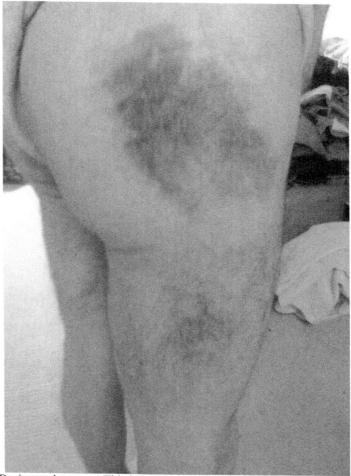

Bruises galore, too. This impressive bruise was despite my wearing padded hip protectors.

Falls are not limited to the home either. This was the result of slipstream caused by a boy racer passing a too close. It was not the only incident, though there haven't been too many. (On all but one occasion, the driver neither slowed down nor stop to see if I was hurt.)

I guess that he just didn't see me!

Annex 2 - Basics of Nichiren Buddhism

Nam-Myoho-Renge-Kyo

Nam-Myoho-Renge-Kyo is what I chant, every morning and evening. It is the basis of my practice. It sounds incredibly simple and too easy that some words in a strange, foreign language could project someone to enlightenment, but it can and in my experience and in that of many others, it certainly does work.

Myoho-Renge-Kyo is the title of the Lotus Sutra, in Chinese. *Nam* means '*respect or dedication to*' in the same sense as in the Welsh national anthem, the phrase '*Pleidiol wyf i'm gwlad*' (meaning '*I pledge myself to my land*') is used. *Nam* has a similar meaning, although much more profound. *Nam-Myoho-Renge-Kyo* together is thus respect or dedication to *Myoho Renge Kyo,* the Mystic Law of the Lotus Sutra.

Myoho is the relationship between life and death, and the relationship between our highest, or Buddha, enlightened state, and our other states of life.

Renge, the lotus flower, which produces both flowers and seeds at the same time and signifies simultaneity of cause and effect at work deep in the life of each of us. We are caught up in this and fundamentally unable to change. The lotus is a beautiful flower that floats on the surface of water, nourished through its roots in the mud. This is a perfect metaphor for our lives as it illustrates the profound working of life where an effect is simultaneous with a cause. The 'mud' in our lives can always be used as a springboard to reveal our highest life state.

Kyo means 'sutra' or teaching, or vibration of our voice and is a reference to the interconnectedness of all phenomena and how our prayers affect people and situations beyond our immediate sphere. It also means thread, or weave and is a metaphor for universal connectiveness.

Applying all the above to daily life and to mine specifically, undoubtedly my bipolar disorder, both cancers and indeed to my FND itself, all could be regarded as sufferings of birth and death. Understanding the simultaneity of cause and effect has enabled me through chanting to cause my Buddhahood to emerge. That is, my practice, spurred by the challenge of my various illnesses, has shown me very clearly that I can achieve a state of Buddhahood or unsurpassed enlightenment in this lifetime. Chanting *Nam-Myoho-Renge-Kyo* is the key to grasping the mystic truth innate in all life. It is an absurdly simple, positive, and successful act.

As of the 13th of May 2021, I had chanted Nam Myoho Renge Kyo for thirty-six years! On this day each year I contact Carol to thank her, we have agreed that I can repay my debt of gratitude to her by introducing her to Buddhism in a future life, when we meet again.

Through this practice I have endured or overcome many things, in particular cancer twice, bipolar affective disorder and the attendant stigma, job losses, diabetes, gall stones, a disastrous first marriage and separation from my son and more. One name for a Buddha is '*he who can endure*'. I am still fighting, every day, now with FND.

I will win, no matter what.

Cause and effect and the nine consciousnesses

In each moment of our lives through what we think, say and do we make causes. Cause and effect are simultaneous and inseparable, so when we make a cause, any cause, a related effect is stored in our lives. In the right circumstances we will experience the related effect. To understand the nature of *Nam-Myoho-Renge-Kyo* you need an appreciation of something called the nine consciousnesses. These may be thought of as layers of existence that constantly operate together to mould and create our lives. Looking at each, the significance of the simultaneity of cause and effect should be apparent.

The first five consciousnesses are the familiar senses of sight, hearing, touch, smell, and taste, or how we take in information to understand what is going on. At birth, even a baby is aware of these. Like the baby we become attached to the world to an extent that it continues to hold our attention yet leaves us in the dark about deeper layers of our consciousness.

As we develop, we learn to recognise what we experience, such as a colour or what feels cold. *This is the sixth consciousness*, or our mind at work. It is how we make sense of the signals received through our senses. The interaction of these first six consciousnesses allows us to go about our activities of daily living.

The seventh consciousness is more self-directed. It is our inner, spiritual world, the store of collected learning or conditioning, experienced as we grow. This enables us to develop a sense of identity, gender, sexuality, tastes, and preferences and so on. Our attachment to a self is distinct and separate from other people and is anchored in this consciousness as is a sense of what we see as right or wrong. The appearance of therapies and counselling, particularly in the West may simply be a response to free themselves from parts of this conditioning.

This is about as far as Western culture generally understands the consciousnesses.

The concept of *an eighth consciousness* is where our internal causes and internal effects, our karma, is stored but not used in daily life.

What indeed is karma and how can we change it into mission, to contribute to harmonious existence of all life? Karma is our personality with profound tendencies impressed in the deepest levels of our life. These extend beyond this existence and shape not only how we started this life, our circumstances from the moment of birth, but continues beyond our death. Buddhism enables us to transform our tendencies to realize our potential in this lifetime and beyond. Karma is in constant flux. We create our present and future by the choices we make. In this light, karma does not encourage resignation but drives us to become a protagonist in the unfolding drama of our life.

The existence of a ***ninth consciousness*** is the fundamental workings of life itself and most definitely is not generally part of Western culture, not the least as it extends throughout the universe. The ninth consciousness is simply *Nam-Myoho-Renge-Kyo* or the Law of life.

If we could but see all nine consciousnesses, we would appreciate the fundamental and inseparable interconnection of all life.

The Ten worlds

Buddhism embraces our entire life-state, including emotions such as joy or suffering. Whilst this may seem to be an interaction between our life and our circumstances, similar conditions experienced by one person as, say, misery may be a source of exhilaration, challenge, and satisfaction to someone else. Rather like supporters of opposing teams watching the same sports match. Through a resilient and accepting inner state, we can resist and even change the most difficult and negative conditions.

What are these ten worlds? Ordered from the least to the most desirable, they are:

Hell – a place of despair where one is overwhelmed by suffering. The positive aspect is that having experienced hell helps us maintain a desire not only to better our own circumstances but gives us empathy and an understanding of the sufferings of others.

Hunger - a state dominated by a deluded desire that never can be satisfied. The positive aspect is that it can be a driving force to improve things. You may hunger, even yearn to see others happy and to fight for peace in the world.

Animality - an instinctive state that encompasses fearing the strong and bullying the weak. The 'law of the jungle'. On the other hand, this state promotes protective instincts, such as that we need more sleep. It may also lead to the wish to preserve oneself or others.

Anger - a state characterized by an unrestrained competitive urge to surpass and dominate others and often used as the pretext of acting for a perceived common good or as a demonstration of wisdom. Anger may be at injustice and give rise to a passion to fight authoritarian behaviour.

These four states together are referred to as the **Four Evil Paths** because of the very destructive negativity that distinguishes them.

Humanity – this is a tranquil, peaceful state marked by an ability to reason and to make calm judgments. It is fundamental to our identity as a human being but can represent a fragile balance that yields easily to any of the Four Evil Paths when confronted with negative conditions. It is also being at peace, calm and reasonable. An opportunity to restore one's energies.

Rapture – Something we know well, the exhilaration at being alive. It is a state of joy, as experienced when desire is fulfilled, or suffering escaped. This is only a temporary state.

With the Four Evil Paths the last two collectively are called the **Six Lower Worlds**. They are reactions to changing external conditions with a lack of true freedom and autonomy.

Which leaves the last four. Buddhism refers to these as the **Four Noble States**. They require effort to be able to live with integrity, freedom, and compassion.

Learning – This is aspiration to enlightenment and is a driving force. However, the state may lead to self-centredness and separation from others.

Realization – This is an ability to perceive, unaided, the true nature of all phenomena. It also may lead to self-centredness and a tendency to use intellect, rather than wisdom, to solve problems.

These two, learning and realisation are sometimes called the *Two Vehicles*, as these are partial enlightenment and free of some delusions. The conditions can be self-absorbed and in Buddhist texts, people of the Two Vehicles often are admonished for their selfishness and complacency.

Bodhisattva –A state of compassion in which we overcome restraints of egotism and work tirelessly for others' welfare. Mahayana Buddhism emphasizes Bodhisattva as an ideal of human behaviour. Sounds good? Well, it may turn to arrogance if you feel superior to those you are helping. Moreover, pouring out your life-force towards the lives of others, without paying attention to your own needs may propel you towards the lower life states.

Buddhahood or *Enlightenment*. A state of completeness and perfect freedom, where one can enjoy a sense of unity with the fundamental life-force of the universe. In Buddhahood everything, including illness, ageing and death, can be experienced as an opportunity for joy and fulfilment. The life-state of Buddhahood makes itself visible through altruistic commitment and actions enacted in the world of Bodhisattva.

In context, a Buddha is simply an ordinary person awakened to the true nature of life and experiencing absolute happiness and freedom within the realities of daily life. Indestructible joy, unlimited wisdom, courage, compassion, creativity, and life force.

Each world contains within it the other nine. Even a heartless villain loves his wife and children. This shows that he has a portion of the Bodhisattva in him. The potential for enlightened wisdom and action or Buddhahood exists even in someone whose life is dominated by the Four Evil Paths.

The reverse is also true. The life-state of Buddhahood is not separate or discontinuous from the other nine worlds. Rather the wisdom, compassion and courage of Buddhahood can transform a tendency toward, say, anger and functions in life. Anger directed by the compassion of Buddhahood and Bodhisattva, can be a driving force to challenge injustice or to transform society.

The purpose of Buddhist practice, to become happy, is achieved by bringing forth a life-state of Buddhahood through which we illuminate our lives, enabling us to forge lasting value from our eternal journey through all the Ten Worlds.

Mutual possession of the Ten Worlds

As I mentioned, each of the Ten Worlds possesses the potential for all the ten within itself as a mutual possession. This means that life is not fixed in one or another of the Ten Worlds but may manifest any of the ten, from Hell to Buddhahood, at any time. While one of the ten is manifest, the other nine are latent or in the state of non-substantiality. The key to this is that everyone in any of the nine worlds possesses a Buddha nature and has the potential to reveal their Buddhahood.

A Buddha possesses all the nine worlds and is not separate or different from 'ordinary' people.

Choosing one's karma - Ganken Ogo

This is a difficult one!

Each of us chooses this life and our karma to demonstrate the usefulness and the power of the mystic law. If we face everyday life with this in mind, everything appears in a different way and every difficulty is only a challenge to overcome, rather than a wall impossible to climb.

This is exactly how I feel about my FND.

Oneness of life and its environment

This provides that life and its environment, though they seem not to be connected, are in fact two phases of one reality. Each of us has our own unique environment. The effects of karma appear in our lives and in our environment because life and environment are two integral aspects.

Matters of Life and Death

Benjamin Franklin observed *"I believe ... that the soul of man is immortal and will be treated with justice in another life, reflecting its conduct in this."*

My Buddhism gives me great solace that, in spite it never being the best thing to happen, when the death of a relative or a friend occurs, there is a comfort to know that life is a continuous string, unbroken from the limitless past and extending into the infinite future. Life is not just the span that we enjoy this time. It is part of an unbroken line.

As cause and effect are simultaneous and inseparable, knowing someone and what you shared is a cause. The effect is that there is no way to avoid meeting them again. Put together and you will see that there is no 'final' separation. Those we have loved (and those we have not loved) come around again in future existences. Each of us will reunite times without number in the future, just as we have been together countless times in the past.

Put another way:

Death is as natural as breathing. It simply marks the end of our short period in our present lifetime, just as birth marks the beginning. Life is not defined by our time her, now. It has (that is, we have) always existed and will continue to exist into infinity. There is no escaping this. When a close friend of mine died a few years ago, I was comforted with the knowledge that at some time, in a new existence,

I will find myself beside Chris, cheering on a Welsh rugby team (hopefully thrashing our traditional 'enemies' the English.) This abiding thought and philosophy also enabled me to accept the untimely passing of another friend, more recently.

We are also here for a purpose. Many people fail to find their true mission in life. I have found mine, though it took over 65 years of trial and error (mostly errors) to recognise it. I am fundamentally and deeply happy, where I am, how I am, right now. I would add that I was shocked and very saddened by the deaths of both my friends. I grieved, in my own way, saying prayers for both of them and for their future happiness and, despite never meet the latter face to face, feeling the immense joy of having known her.

Yes, life is so hard. I have quoted this elsewhere, but it is particularly relevant. President John F. Kennedy said: *"we do this not because it is easy, we do it because it is hard."*

So, by all means weep, regret and grieve. This is a completely natural, human reaction. But take solace in that we will meet again.

Why me? The purpose of illness and suffering

Often members of the FND Hope Facebook support groups voice the question: '*Why me?*' or '*What did I do to deserve this?*' or '*Why does this keep happening in my life?*'

This is a very natural but ultimately a rather futile question. Our karma is so profound over this and many previous lifetimes that it is quite impossible to work out what causes you may have made in the past that are producing today's effects in your life.

'Why?' is a negative, backward-looking question. Much healthier is to look at the <u>how's</u> of a solution rather than the <u>why's</u> of the problem. There is a third approach. Nichiren Buddhism reveals that it is far healthier to regard '<u>why me?</u>' as the positive, forward-looking question.

If you see your present problems (or 'heavily disguised gifts') you are encouraged to chant about your future (or visualise it, if you're not a Buddhist) and begin your answer not by looking over your shoulder with a *'because I did...'* or a *'because I am'* attitude, but with a forward looking *'so that I can...'*. Then your own boundless and barely tapped reservoir of wisdom will launch the insight necessary to complete the answer:

"So that I can... be more compassionate/learn to love my parents or partner/fulfil my full potential at work/treasure my health/find a relationship based on deep respect...', and so on.

In Buddhism this is called 'transforming karma into mission'. It harnesses suffering to strengthen a sense of purpose. This, however long and painful it may feel, turns you into the architect of your own future, rather than your staying as a victim of your past.

'Mission' here does not necessarily mean finding some far-flung idea of a destiny to discover new planets, or a noble calling to work with the disadvantaged in the third world, although either of these things may be in your future if you decide it. Instead, it indicates a strong sense of purpose and a sense of responsibility to guide your every day, steer your choices and actions, and reveal your unique individual talents. These will help you to make a positive difference in society.

One of the most potent and important symbols in Nichiren Buddhism is the beautiful lotus flower which grows only in a muddy pond of daily life.

Endpiece

If all this has not entirely put you off ever reading more of my self-indulgent scribblings, you may be interested to read one or more of my eleven romantic novels, available on Amazon Kindle, in a series called Take Four Girls.

Be warned, none has any literary merit but mark my self-indulgence and belief that I might be capable of writing a novel or two.

- *Take Four Girls*
- *Mary's Baby*
- *One fewer lass*
- *One more lass*
- *Raglan Way*
- *Another Long Ride*
- *Trainee Surgeon*
- *Two Yachts*
- *Pog's Long ride*
- *Back Again*
- Positively the final episode (I promise): *More From ...*

I also wrote another forgettable book, called *Christmas Crackers – How to Survive the Office Christmas Party*, which may be of some use and guidance for the innocent or not yet initiated into the horrors of this annual corporate career limiting minefield!

With the pandemic restrictions and the shenanigans surrounding the alleged party at No 10 Downing Street in December 2020, which allegedly didn't happen, but all the rules were followed, I think that a revision will appear in 2022.

I also have an account of my tussle with throat cancer in 2006. It is under the title of *Nobody told the Bumblebee*.

END

Printed in Great Britain
by Amazon

82712357R00081